Career Counselling

Robert Nathan & Linda Hill

SAGE Publications
London • Newbury Park • New Delhi

First published 1992

SAGE Publications Ltd
6 Bonhill Street
London EC2A 4PU

SAGE Publications Inc
2455 Teller Road
Newbury Park, California 91320

SAGE Publications India Pvt Ltd
32, M-Block Market
Greater Kailash – I
New Delhi 110 048

British Library Cataloguing in Publication Data

Nathan, Robert
  Career Counselling. – (Counselling in Practice Series)
  I. Title II. Hill, Linda III. Series
  361.323

  ISBN 0–8039–8695–5
  ISBN 0–8039–8696–3 (pbk)

Library of Congress catalog card number 92–056427

Typeset by Mayhew Typesetting, Rhayader, Powys
Printed in Great Britain by Biddles Ltd, Guildford, Surrey

Career
Counselling

Counselling in Practice

Series editor: Windy Dryden
Associate editor: E. Thomas Dowd

Counselling in Practice is a series of books developed especially for counsellors and students of counselling which provides practical, accessible guidelines for dealing with clients with specific, but very common, problems.

Counselling Survivors of Childhood Sexual Abuse
Claire Burke Draucker

Counselling with Dreams and Nightmares
Delia Cushway and Robyn Sewell

Counselling for Depression
Paul Gilbert

Counselling for Anxiety Problems
Richard Hallam

Career Counselling
Robert Nathan and Linda Hill

Counselling for Post-traumatic Stress Disorder
Michael J. Scott and Stephen G. Stradling

Counselling for Alcohol Problems
Richard Velleman

Contents

To my parents, who gave me such a
good start in life.

LH

To my daughters Louise and
Deborah, who will always be
special to me whatever careers
they choose.

RN

Acknowledgements

We are very grateful to the following people for their help and encouragement during the preparation of the book. In particular, we want to thank Jean Floyed for her perceptive and intelligent comments; Michal Peleg and Chris Bell for reading the final draft; Marilyn Goodman and Jenny Nathan for reading early drafts and for their support; and of course Windy Dryden for asking us to write the book and for his incisive editing.

1

Introduction

People think I'm successful. I'm well paid, have a nice house and I'm good at my job. But I feel more and more dissatisfied with what I do.

I can't take a year off. How will it look on my CV? Employers will think I've been wasting my time.

Everyone's telling me I've got a lot of potential; but I've lost interest in studying.

When I married Sam, I thought he would be such a good provider. Now he's been made redundant.

The key words in these statements – successful, wasting, potential, provider, redundant – reflect a valuing of success and achievement. It is hardly surprising, therefore, that many people who approach a career counsellor, influenced by this pressure to succeed, may feel to some degree a failure in the eyes of partners, peers, employers or parents.

These assumptions, influences and values raise a number of considerations for career counsellors. Our clients may want to turn their feelings of failure into a successful solution fairly urgently – to put things *right*, to find the *right* career, to feel all *right*. Their need to get things right may be transferred into expectations of the career counselling process to come up with the right answer, and to focus on extrinsic aspects of job satisfaction, such as money, status and working conditions, rather than considering their personal strengths and weaknesses.

Additional external pressures, such as keeping up the mortgage payments, saving face with friends or getting into the best college course tend to discourage clients from addressing any personal, and perhaps painful emotional issues. These include understanding, accepting and building on changes in personal values; and coping with any negative feelings, such as the loss and anger so often felt after losing a job.

What is career counselling?

Most people, if asked to define career counselling, are likely to believe that it resembles the approach proposed by Parsons, as long ago as 1909. He wrote:

> In the wise choice of vocation, there are three factors.
> 1. A clear understanding of yourself
> 2. A knowledge of the requirements and prospects in different lines of work
> 3. True reasoning on the relations of these two groups of facts.

This approach is based on the measurement, through testing, of the client's aptitudes and interests, followed by a recommendation by an 'expert' on occupations which provide a match in terms of the aptitudes and interests required. This process of 'talent matching' (sometimes known as the 'test and tell' approach) was the predominant form of assistance available to people seeking career help until the 1960s. For a number of reasons, we believe that career counsellors should not accept their clients' demands and expectations for 'advice on the best career'.

First, making appropriate occupational decisions needs the assistance of skilled and sensitive counselling: to reach the point where a rational decision can be made, emotional issues such as managing relationships, coping with loss and change and recovering from damaged self-esteem may first have to be addressed.

Secondly, since a 'job for life' is no longer a reality, lifelong decision-making skills are more conducive to the continuing challenge of making appropriate life and occupational choices, which themselves are increasingly interdependent.

Thirdly, employers require an increasingly flexible approach to their changing requirements, expecting employees to take responsibility for managing their own development, which might mean creating or accepting a 'development opportunity', such as a secondment, rather than waiting for promotion. There is also an increasing recognition that individuals themselves progress through a number of life stages (Super, 1980) and changes in their role requirements and responsibilities (Herriot, 1992).

Fourthly, making decisions is very much a matter of personal responsibility. A counselling approach empowers people to take such responsibility where they, not the counsellor, are the 'expert'.

The career counsellor, like all other counsellors, provides time, support, attention, skill and a structure which enables clients to become more aware of their own resources in order to lead a more satisfying life. We see career counselling as *a process which enables people to recognise and utilise their resources to make career-*

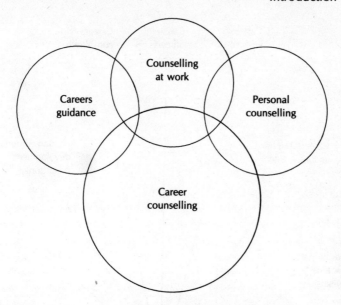

Figure 1.1 *How career counselling overlaps with other forms of help*

related decisions and manage career-related problems. Although focusing on the work-related part of a person's life, it also takes into account the interdependence of career and non-career considerations.

This book focuses on the practice of career counselling. Figure 1.1 illustrates how career counselling overlaps with other kinds of counselling and careers guidance.

'Counselling-at-Work' refers to the set of counselling activities offered by employers for their employees, and may address work- or non-work-related problems, including concerns regarding career satisfaction. Such counselling services are sometimes known as Employee Assistance Programmes (EAPs). Their scope is described in Megranahan (1989).

The term 'guidance' is commonly used in the UK to mean 'help for individuals to make choices about education, training and employment' (Hawthorn, 1991). Practitioners who offer help with career choices often describe this work as careers (or vocational) guidance. This is somewhat confusing as the term 'guidance' has connotations of directive, prescriptive help. In fact 'guidance' is an umbrella term which encompasses counselling as well as activities such as informing, coaching, teaching, assessment and advocacy.

In addressing personal concerns regarding redundancy, retraining,

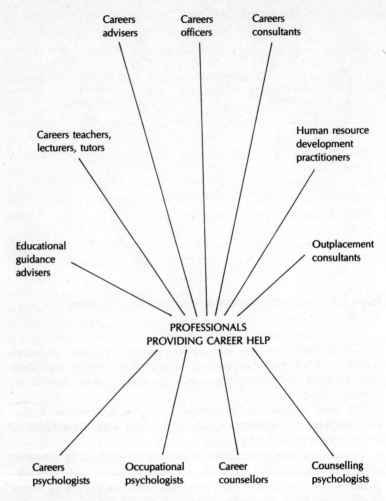

Figure 1.2 *Who provides career help?*

relocation, retirement, relationships at work, promotion, career breaks and stress, career counselling necessarily overlaps with personal counselling.

The provision of career counselling
Unfortunately, in the UK the provision for adults seeking career help is very patchy and largely uncoordinated, and much of what does exist is neither informed by a counselling ethos nor staffed by people who are trained in a counselling approach. Help for young

people in making career decisions is offered nationally by careers teachers in schools and professionally qualified careers officers employed by the local authority careers service. Government-backed career help for adults is not available on a national basis in the same comprehensive, independent and professional way.

The various professionals involved in helping others to face career dilemmas are shown in Figure 1.2.

There are some careers services which offer help to adults as well as young people. Universities and polytechnics have careers advisers who provide independent help, which is usually free of charge. However, the service is restricted to people who are graduating from their courses.

Parts of the country have services for the general public which offer information on learning opportunities. Since many people look for courses when they are seeking a career change, the educational guidance provided by these services overlaps to some extent with career counselling (see Edwards, 1989). Some agencies which provide educational or training courses, for example colleges of further education, adult education institutes and Training and Enterprise Councils, also offer guidance to any adult, but as this is part of a marketing exercise it is unlikely to be independent.

The Employment Department offers a number of programmes (currently known as Restart and JobClubs) through which adults can receive free and independent guidance, but these programmes are restricted to the long-term unemployed.

Some employers offer career help to their staff, for example, career development workshops for women, help with job hunting for people who are being made redundant, retirement planning services, and career counselling sessions with a personnel officer. However, clearly there are difficulties involved in providing help which is independent and client centred rather than organisation centred.

Some national organisations, for example, the Armed Forces, the Law Society and the Royal National Institute for the Blind, also offer career help to special groups.

Because career counselling provision for adults in the UK has been so sparsely resourced by the government, there has been a mushrooming of independent services, staffed by specialist career counsellors, occupational psychologists and counselling psychologists, for people with career-related dissatisfactions. These services differ in their use of psychometric tests. There are some services which still offer a 'test and tell' approach, in which the client is given a series (or 'battery') of tests measuring aptitudes, occupational interests and aspects of personality, the results of which are then interpreted by a consultant psychologist and a report with recommendations subsequently written. Other career counsellors may make no use of tests, but use counselling skills to assist clients in focusing on occupational and other aspects of their lives. Still others will use a combination of assessment and counselling, with a greater or lesser emphasis on one or the other.

Outplacement consultants offer specific help to executives and others facing a job loss. This may involve some counselling to assist recovery from the trauma of the redundancy, but more usually focuses on coaching and support in job hunting. Such services are often paid for by the company as part of a severance package.

Confusingly, some practitioners who describe themselves as career counsellors are not doing career counselling in the sense that they subscribe to a counselling philosophy or have training in counselling skills.

Although traditionally offered on a one-to-one basis, career counselling is increasingly being offered in groups. There are a number of advantages of working in groups:

- Participants realise that they are not alone – others are facing similar issues.
- Mutual support is readily available both during and after the group's existence.
- A group provides a wider range of resources, ideas and information.
- There is less dependency on the counsellor as 'expert'.
- Groups provide more opportunities to use active techniques such as coaching in job-hunting skills.
- They are economical to run.

Many such groups are run within employing organisations, and may be focused primarily on occupational issues, more broadly on life and career development, or may be part of a positive action programme, for example, directed at women or black people. Some independent agencies offer career and life-review workshops, whilst there is government backing for projects to assist the long-term unemployed to assess their job-related skills and receive support and coaching in job hunting. A combination of group and individual approaches may be used as part of a career counselling programme. For example, the administration of psychometric tests can be done in a group, followed by individual feedback and counselling, followed by interview practice in a group. Most of the approaches and techniques described in this book are amenable to either a one-to-one or a group approach.

There are a number of career counselling-related activities which are increasingly used in organisations, including mentoring, development centres and self-help tools. For a detailed review of the practice of career counselling in organisations, see Jackson (1990), which describes a plethora of activities falling under the banner of career counselling.

Box 1.1 summarises the services which professional career counsellors may offer.

Box 1.1   *The services which may be offered by career counsellors*

One-to-one career counselling:
  one-off consultation;
  a series of one-to-one meetings without assessment;
  a series of one-to-one meetings with test administration, feedback and counselling;
  a series of career counselling meetings with written assignments (but no tests);
  a series of career counselling meetings with tests and written assignments.

Group career counselling:
  Career development workshops (also known by other titles, such as career planning or review workshops, or self-development groups)

Access to a careers library

Access to computerised occupational information and self-help careers guidance tools

Coaching in job-hunting techniques, including CV writing and interview practice: this may be one-to-one or group based

---

The majority of career counsellors provide their clients with access to careers information in some form. An approach to occupational information which is consistent with a counselling ethos is examined in detail in Chapter 5. Some career counsellors make use of computerised occupational information and other careers guidance tools. This is a specialised topic for which there is no space in this book, although Appendices C and D refer to useful resources. Job-hunting techniques are not the domain of this book, but are detailed in Floyed and Nathan (1991).

Who should read this book?

This book will assist specialist career counsellors and advisers who offer career counselling as their main work role. The skills and techniques will also be of value to other practitioners who encounter people who need help in choosing, changing or developing their careers. Practising counsellors and psychotherapists, whether they are working with individuals or groups, will find the structured approach and the specific occupational considerations of benefit when a job-related concern is affecting a client's well-being. Other professionals who use career counselling skills and techniques, or who offer career counselling within another role, will find the book a thorough and practical guide to the process of career counselling and the different techniques available. This group includes personnel and training managers, recruitment and outplacement consultants, careers officers and educational guidance advisers, who may need to assist staff and clients in addressing career-related issues as part of their role. For the sake of simplicity and clarity, throughout the book we refer to 'career counsellors' to cover both categories.

Although the main focus is on work with adults, the book will also be valuable to anyone helping young people to make occupational decisions. Ball (1984) focuses more specifically on careers work with young people. This book is a manual, not an exposition of theory. A detailed consideration of career choice and development theories will be found in Arthur et al. (1989).

Our approach to career counselling

Taylor (1985) has identified a number of critical questions applicable to the practice of career counselling.

To what extent should the client's feelings be expressed and dealt with, or is the focus on the rational aspects of decision making? It is unrealistic to expect that all clients will be ready to consider rationally the choices available. Career counselling should allow clients' feelings to be expressed where such expression will further the goals of career counselling.

For some people, the degree of anxiety felt about a work or non-work problem will need to be addressed either prior to or concurrent with career counselling. For example, a divorcée may need to address feelings of loss while seeking to support herself financially.

For other people, various 'self-defeating beliefs' may be contributing to unproductive behaviour not only in making rational decisions about a career, but also at work (see Chapter 4).

Who should collect or provide the information – client, counsellor or both? We believe that this is a joint responsibility. The two main types of information the client needs in order to make an occupational decision are (1) information about him or herself, and (2) information about occupations.

Our practice is to make use of various sources of information about a client, including self-assessment exercises, psychometric tests, and information emerging from discussion in counselling sessions. Both the counsellor and the client are information collectors, although the collection belongs to the client.

Regarding information about occupations, our contract is that the client is responsible for researching information about occupations, whilst the counsellor points the client towards sources (see Chapter 5).

Who is the expert (that is, who should be in charge, deciding how the problems raised should be handled) – the client, counsellor or both? We believe that clients are very much the experts as far as handling their own problems is concerned. It can be easy for clients to give up their power to the career counsellor, and adopt a passive approach to the 'expert advice giver'. We like to involve clients in choosing whether to take tests, and by completing homework assignments, listening to and reflecting upon tape recordings of feedback discussions and researching options. Whilst some counsellors and clients may have misgivings about the tape recording of sessions, we have found this to be a powerful tool consistent with the values of counselling (see Chapter 5).

Who should have the responsibility for making the decision – client or counsellor? What we are describing in this book is an approach to career counselling firmly rooted in a counselling, not a didactic or advisory, ethos. The responsibility for decision making is therefore with the client, whilst the counsellor is responsible for facilitating the process.

What should the predominant counsellor style be – directive, collaborative, interpretive or reflective? Career counsellors need to be able to adapt their styles according to the needs of the client and the stage of the career counselling process. A prescriptive or directive style is inappropriate to the approach described in this book.

A reflective style may well be appropriate early in the career counselling, but may also be appropriate together with tentative interpretations and a more confronting style later on. In the final stages of career counselling, when action is possibly being addressed, a reinforcing style may be appropriate. At such times, we might use an informative approach, giving clients access to new knowledge. We see the entire career counselling process as facilitating clients' resources to manage their careers more effectively. Since many clients who come for individual career counselling undervalue their strengths and skills, we also use a supportive style to affirm their intrinsic value. When it is appropriate, we would also use a cathartic style, enabling clients to free themselves from negative emotions through, for example, crying and expressing anger. See Heron (1990) for a fuller discussion on styles of intervention.

What should be discussed in career counselling? The client's personal/emotional problems, self-appraisal, decision making, tests results, information on options, evaluating options?   Our approach recognises the interdependence of problems and that personal issues need to be addressed within the career counselling process. The question of when personal counselling is more appropriate than career counselling is addressed in Chapter 7.

Summary of the contents
In Chapter 2 we shall examine the kinds of difficulties and dilemmas that clients commonly bring to career counselling. These include problems associated with particular life stages and events; the balance between work and non-work aspects of life; difficulties in making or implementing career decisions; problems brought about by change in organisations, and performance-related issues. In each case, we indicate the kind of concerns presented, any underlying problems and the implications for career counsellors.

The next four chapters are concerned with the stages in the career counselling process, which are summarised in Box 1.2.

If clients are thoroughly briefed about the nature of the service, and can decide for themselves whether career counselling is appropriate, they are more likely to gain from the career counselling than if they had arrived with little or no preparation. Chapter 3 addresses the important but often underemphasised screening and contracting stages, during which the client can become clear about what to expect from career counselling, and the counsellor can explore the likelihood of being able to help this person meet his or her expectations. An initial meeting can be used as a preliminary

Box 1.2   Stages of career counselling

Stage	Client tasks	Counsellor tasks
Screening, contracting, exploring	Making a preliminary assessment of the suitability of career counselling. Undertaking written preparation. Testing out readiness for and appropriateness of career counselling. Exploring presenting concerns and influences on career and educational choices. Clarifying expectations of career counselling. Discussing and agreeing contract.	Educating and informing clients about career counselling. Evaluating the client's readiness for and appropriateness of career counselling. Suggesting more suitable forms of help, if necessary. Building rapport. Facilitating exploration. Establishing contract (i.e. confidentiality, structure etc.).
Enabling client's understanding	Considering the questions: 'Who am I? Where am I now? What do I want? Where do I want to be?' Completing self-assessment exercises, psychometric tests and questionnaires, as appropriate. Being prepared to tackle the question 'What's stopping me?' Researching occupational information.	Facilitating exploration of feelings and beliefs associated with career problem/concern. Helping client to identify important themes and integrate self-understanding. Making appropriate use of self-assessment exercises and psychometric tests and questionnaires. Helping client to overcome blocks to action, using challenging skills, if appropriate. Signposting occupational information for the client.
Action and endings	Completing decision-making and action planning exercises. Developing options and choosing between options. Putting decision into action. Agreeing research tasks, if appropriate. Addressing fears of change. Evaluating need for continued support. Reviewing progress made towards objectives during career counselling.	Enabling clients to develop options and choose between them. Supporting client in developing action plan. Agreeing research tasks, if appropriate. Helping clients face ambivalence about the future. Exploring client's need for continued support. Stressing importance of maintaining momentum. Helping client to identify resources and sources of support.

discussion, without full commitment on either side, and can fulfil a number of purposes:

● It allows clients to 'opt out' without further commitment.
● It enables career counsellors to evaluate the readiness of clients for career counselling.
● It educates clients about the career counselling process, beyond any written documentation.
● It allows both counsellor and client to discuss the most appropriate 'contract', including the usefulness of assessment tests for this person.

The development of self-understanding is central to Chapters 4 and 5. Chapter 4 looks at the process of enabling clients to address the questions: 'Who am I?'; 'What do I want?' and 'What is stopping me?' For some clients, greater self-understanding is all that is needed, and this may promote new energy or a change of attitude. For others, self-understanding is just the first stage. They want career counselling to help them make decisions or formulate action plans. Chapter 4 also addresses the crucial stage between promoting self-understanding and taking action – that of enabling clients to reduce the effects of any blocks to action. In particular, we look at the importance of assisting clients to evaluate the impact of self-defeating beliefs and values.

Chapter 5 presents many techniques which career counsellors can use to promote self-understanding in their clients, and describes how these techniques, including between-sessions homework assignments, psychometric tests and questionnaires and occupational information, can be woven into career counselling. Tests can be appropriate and beneficial if they are administered sensitively and at the right point in the career counselling. If tests are given together with other tools, such as interest questionnaires and self-assessment exercises, they contribute towards, but do not dominate, any feedback discussions. All 'data' which are produced during the career counselling process can be of value. Data may include written preparation by clients, feedback by the counsellor and responses by clients to such feedback.

Many counselling practitioners find it hard to enable their clients to move on from the exploration and clarification stages of the career counselling process to the 'decision-making' and 'action' stages, where these are appropriate. In Chapter 6, practical techniques of encouraging clients to make and follow through their decisions are described. These include exercises for 'choosing between options', completing 'action plans' and addressing fears of change.

Chapter 6 also considers the value of 'follow-up', an aspect of career counselling which is often overlooked.

The boundary between career and personal counselling, the question of referral, and working with 'third parties' such as employers or partners are some of the key issues for career counsellors which are explored in Chapter 7. Career counsellors need general counselling skills. These are summarised in this chapter, together with a description of some of the areas of specialist knowledge which career counsellors need, for example, an understanding of factors relevant in career management.

Like all counsellors, career counsellors must maintain good professional practice in order to maximise the quality of the service provided, the protection of clients and their own well-being. The elements of monitoring and evaluation, non-managerial supervision and counsellor self-management are described in Chapter 8.

The book is illustrated throughout with case study examples which are derived from individuals who have presented their concerns to a career counsellor. Names and identifying material have been changed to safeguard client confidentiality.

2
Issues in Career Counselling

Individuals approach career counselling when they have identified issues in their lives which they perceive to be primarily *career*-related, and therefore appropriate for discussion with a career counsellor. However, we believe it naive and unrealistic to help clients solve their *career* problems without allowing them to see the wider ramifications of their situation. In order to find the best solution to a career-related issue, we often find that clients need to examine their career problem in the context of their lives as a whole. This may be necessary for the following reasons:

- The desire for a more interesting job may be a reflection of a life stage or event outside of work.
- Problems can be linked (for example, a relationship difficulty at home may have precipitated a crisis at work).
- A long-time problem which has been tolerated may have become intolerable (for example, continuing relationship difficulties at work may have been tolerated until a 'last straw' incident).
- Lack of career advancement may be partly linked to poor interpersonal skills.
- Anger towards 'company policy' may reflect a general dislike, for example of being controlled.
- An apparently realistic constraint (for example, a recession) may belie the need to focus on the emotions engendered by personal difficulties.
- Dissatisfaction with job content or career attainment may conceal a deeper lack of self-esteem.

This chapter will discuss the kinds of client who come for career counselling, the problems they typically bring, the issues which may sometimes underlie the presenting problems, and the implications for the practice of career counselling.

First, we discuss problems which may be typical of a certain stage or time of life, for example the 'mid-life crisis'. We then examine work–life balance issues, inability to make a career decision, difficulty in implementing a choice, problems arising from change at work (including redundancy), performance problems, relationship problems, and issues connected with creativity. These categories are not of course mutually exclusive, and many clients will need help with problems in several categories.

An individual or common problem?

Clients coming for career counselling may be helped initially by receiving written literature detailing the kinds of problem commonly brought. This in itself can reduce a sense of isolation ('I'm not the only one') and allow an early airing of the problem. Box 2.1 shows some of the common questions asked of career counsellors.

Box 2.1 *Common questions which clients bring to career counselling*

- I feel at a crossroads in my career. Can you help me decide which way to go?
- I am shortly to be made redundant. Can you help me plan my future?
- I think I know what I want, but I can't seem to motivate myself. Can you help me explore what might be holding me back?
- I haven't worked for several years. Can you help me assess my true strengths and build up my confidence?
- I have growing feelings of dissatisfaction with my career. Can you help me reflect on the suitability of the career I have chosen?
- I'm not happy in my current job. But I am not sure whether I should change careers, or just need a change of employer. Can you help me decide?
- Nothing seems to interest me or excite me. I'm at a loss.
- I'm interested in so many things. Can you help me focus?

Every client coming for career counselling brings a unique response to whatever problems he or she is facing. A fundamental principle of any counselling intervention is that clients are allowed to find their own unique solution to a problem, *even if the problem being faced is a common one.*

Career counsellors must recognise that an individual's needs, aspirations and career opportunities are affected by factors like gender, class, race, disability and age. For example, although there are some general principles to be borne in mind in counselling a client who has been made redundant, it is important for a career counsellor working with a black woman who has been made redundant to be sensitive to how her feelings and experiences as a woman and as a black person affect her situation.

Thomas (1990) suggests the following questions for counsellors:

1   What is the ostensible problem that brings the client to counselling, and how common is this problem within the client's age group, gender group and cultural group?
2   Among people of this client's age, gender and cultural type, what other problems and conditions are often linked to, or underlie, the client's apparent problem?
3   How many attitudes that are held by society towards people of the client's age, gender and cultural type influence such a client's problem? Furthermore, how free is the client to choose what ambitions, lifestyles and methods of personal/social adjustment he or she will adopt?
4   How can the level of physical, cognitive, emotional and social development of clients at this life stage, of this gender and of this cultural type help determine the counselling techniques that are likely to be most suitable?

However, Thomas suggests that career counsellors should be wary of trying to fit their clients into 'normal' groups, and risk losing sight of that particular person's individuality – it is that individuality which provides clients with the energy needed to make decisions and manage their problems:

> While descriptive group data can suggest questions to pose and areas of counselees' lives to investigate, the success of treating any case depends ultimately on how artfully the counselor discovers – by means of interviews, observations, tests and intuition – how the variables in each client's life are woven together to form that person's special pattern of individuality. (Thomas, 1990)

Clients often come to career counselling feeling that they 'ought' to be different in some way from how they actually are; their individuality has not been allowed to flourish. Some of these feelings stem from parental values which have been internalised, so that people try to conform to or live up to parental expectations. For example, a classical education at a boys' public school paid for by parents who want their son to enter a profession puts one set of pressures on a person, quite different from the pressures placed on a girl with a mother who has played a traditional homemaking role and whose schooling has channelled her into taking secretarial studies. Carl Rogers describes the imposition of 'conditions of worth' on a child by parents. He defines a fully functioning person as a person who is fully open to experience, with access to all the available data in a situation, and who is free to 'discover that course of action which would come closest to satisfying all his needs in that situation' (Rogers, 1965). Conditions of worth limit the natural development and unfolding of potential and personality, and stunt or slant a person's development in various ways. When people do not live up to parental expectations (whether through trying but failing, or through rebellion) feelings of failure and confusion are often engendered.

Conditions of worth also arise from societal values which have been internalised. The power structures in society define some groups of people as second-class citizens, which affects the self-esteem and individuality of people in those groups. Discrimination, usually indirect, exists (in spite of legislation, in some cases), and operates against the aspirations of people from these 'minorities'. The following case study shows how, even if people from 'minority' groups are not actively discriminated against in education or employment, they may compare themselves with the 'norm' and feel a failure:

Mary had gone to a very traditional girls' grammar school. Her father was a manual worker and her mother served in a cake shop, and they lived on a council estate. Although Mary did well at school and stayed on to study for A levels, she never thought she was clever enough to go to university. No one in her family had ever been, and Mary didn't bother applying. She left school with three good A-level passes during a recession and was unemployed for several months before finding a clerical job in a small company. She did well there, but found the work boring. At the age of 26, after some encouragement from her boyfriend, she decided to apply for a part-time degree course in law. Her father couldn't understand why she wanted to do the course, saying, 'You've got a good job already'. Mary was offered a place, and intended to begin that autumn. However, at the last minute she found she was quite unable to bring herself to go along to the course.

Through career counselling, Mary realised that her feelings about coming from a 'council background' were giving rise to ambivalence about doing the course. She remembered that when she had started at the grammar school, some of the girls had called her 'common', sneered at her accent and her clothing and joked about her mother working in the local cake shop. The parents of these girls were from the professional classes. At some level Mary felt that law degrees were only for middle-class people, and that she was 'not good enough'. She expressed a strong fear that she would be 'found out'.

Even if discrimination and oppression ended today, career counsellors would face a 'backlog' for many years to come of individuals from 'minority' groups who have experienced discrimination in education and employment, in addition to the negative effects of oppression which, like Mary, people have internalised. Some guidelines for career counsellors when working with clients who are from 'minority' groups are given in Chapter 7.

Within this framework, we will now consider the people who come for career counselling, and the common problems they bring.

Life stage problems

Life stages, and their associated tasks, were identified as far back as 2,500 years ago, as quoted in *The Sayings of the Fathers* (The Talmud). Fourteen ages of man were indicated, each with its own developmental tasks. More recently, Shakespeare outlined seven ages of man in *As You Like It*. Since the 1970s, there has been a plethora of stage theories, the most influential including Levinson et al. (1978), Super (1957, 1980) and Sheehy (1976). Certain myths have probably developed about the kind of tasks, attitudes and behaviours *expected* of people in each stage. For example, men in their forties are supposed to go through the 'male menopause'. Such myths can act as an unhelpful pressure; if young adults under the age of 25 are supposed to be high in drive to succeed, or people in their late twenties are expected to be 'settling down', clients who find themselves with a low desire to achieve at 22 or a desire to travel at 29 may feel guilty for feeling different from what is expected of them, or they might think that something is wrong with them. In this section we look at six life stages and some of the associated career counselling issues.

School leavers
The concerns for school leavers revolve around 'what next?' The relatively unknown world of work or further study awaits young people. They want knowledge and guidance, but they are also going through an important transition from the structured lifestyle in school to the less structured world outside.

Many young people will be subject to influences from parents and peers, and will be trying to establish their own meaning and identity out of these perhaps conflicting influences. For example, Jonathan's parents had hoped that he would go on to university. But his friends were leaving school at 16, and going directly into jobs. Their purchasing power was substantial compared to his. Jonathan did quite poorly in his A levels, and came for career counselling at the behest of his parents.

From our experience of working with young people, it is important to establish a contract clearly and directly with the young person. Contracting is covered in more detail in Chapter 3. Additionally, the nature of the referral can tell the career counsellor something of the problem and the client's relationship to the problem. This is further discussed in Chapter 7.

The twenties

People in this age band are faced with the task of finally leaving the parental home and establishing their own individual identity. This time of life usually involves some 'trying out' of different jobs, and clients may bring to career counselling their 'first job blues'. Problems may have arisen owing to difficulties experienced in adjusting to the requirements of the job. Questions such as, 'Is this really what work is about?' may be on the agenda. Disappointment with the values and ethos of the work environment may be combined with a sense of loss for school or college.

Confusion concerning the boundaries of their competence may surface: 'I did well in school, but I wasn't prepared for this.' Fitting in socially may also be a consideration.

Age 30 transition

This is a common stage for people to seek career counselling, as it is a time of questioning the values and decisions of the twenties. Careers and relationships are particularly liable for reassessment. People may realise that they have drifted or been pushed into a career path. Now, they want to take more control of their life and career direction. The consideration of settling down with a partner and family may be an issue, whether or not the person wants it, and the age 30 transition can be a particularly difficult time for women. Clients are often more prepared to reflect on their initial commitments than they might have been a few years earlier.

The thirties

Many of our clients in their thirties are 'waking up' to their own mortality. The expectation of this stage is that people will want to be more settled into a career, a relationship and a particular lifestyle. Those clients who are not conforming to this expectation, either by choice or otherwise, may bring an additional sense of failure to career counselling.

Clients who are conforming to this expectation may want help with making solid plans for the future. Some may not be progressing in their chosen career as quickly as they would like and want assistance in understanding why this may be so. Others may be having difficulty in managing relationships at work, and want to review their personal strengths and weaknesses, rather than just their suitability for certain careers. The particular choice may be to develop their careers into management or to stay in a more technical, specialised function.

Midlife transition

This can be a most confused time of life. It brings a sense of physical decline. With increasing age, the length of retraining required, financial and personal commitments and the perceived difficulties of adjusting to a new lifestyle, the prospect of a second or even third career seems increasingly difficult to attain. In spite of outward signs of success, the person approaching the career counsellor may feel a sense of emptiness – a lack of fulfilment. There may be an acute recognition of the gap between early aspirations and actual achievements. There may be a concern to do something 'more worthwhile'. Career counsellors could be asked to help clients recover their 'spark'.

For some women, this may be a time when, after bringing up their children, they want to return to a full-time career. Career counsellors could be asked to give help with assessing capabilities, restoring confidence and, in particular, looking at transferable skills.

Collin (1979) discusses the symptoms and causes of the so-called 'mid-life crisis'. For many people, it can be an opportunity for development, growth and fulfilment – see Bailey (1982) and Clay (1989) for case studies which demonstrate this.

Forty-five plus

The possibiity or reality of redundancy can hit people particularly hard in this stage of life. Reactions will depend on the person's expectation of re-employment, financial and personal support and previous sense of self-worth.

The prospect of retirement begins to emerge now. Some people may want to consider developing new, or reviving old, interests. The stereotype of 'slowing down' may be a concern for someone who is wanting to begin a new career. The prospect of an abrupt shift to leisure may cause fear or apprehension in some people, whereas with increased life expectancies, the post-retirement period should perhaps be seen much more positively as a 'Third Age' in which people can continue to grow and develop (Schuller and Walker, 1990).

Some clients may want help in 'making sense of' or coming to terms with their past decisions so that they can more smoothly pass on to the next stage of their lives.

Implications for career counsellors

Life stage theory can be useful to career counsellors in considering the possibility of age-related issues being relevant to clients, but it should not become a straitjacket for neatly pigeonholing a person. Rather, a mental note can be made of possible areas of concern to the client at this time in his or her life. No stage theory can interpret how an individual reacts to a particular situation.

Normal age-related problems are sometimes mistaken as signs of serious emotional disturbance. According to Moreland (1979), cycles of stability interspersed with crisis are natural to human development and should not be considered pathological. Information about life stages can come as a great relief to clients.

The consideration of how a person's values might be changing according to their life stage is an important one for career counsellors. Values also change as a result of events or experiences in the individual's life. Box 2.2 summarises some situations which can cause an individual to rethink his or her values.

Box 2.2 *Life events affecting values*

- Bereavement
- Redundancy
- Divorce
- Long-term unemployment
- Injury or disease causing temporary or permanent disability
- Recovery from alcoholism or other addiction
- Recovery from mental illness
- Return home after long period of travel
- Returning to 'civilian life' after a period in uniformed service
- Birth of children
- Children leaving home

Problems to do with work–life balance

Some clients who want to resolve career problems may do so simply by making a change in their employer, job or career. Others, however, may want or need to review how their work fits into the rest of their lives. Issues about work–life balance often arise for clients who are going through life transitions, or who have, or are considering having, children:

> Laura had been working in a routine clerical job for ten years, since she left school; work had held very little significance for her. She was referred for career counselling by a bereavement counsellor, following the death of her husband. She now needed more satisfaction from her work.

> Tariq worked long, anti-social hours in the catering industry. With two small children, he was beginning to feel that he was missing out on family life, and wanted a job which would allow him a better balance between work and family.

> Althea had brought up two boys and a girl and had never worked outside the home. At the age of 36, she now wanted to get a job.

> Malcolm was a self-employed builder, married to a nurse. After they had their first child, Malcolm's wife said she would like to go back to work and develop her career. His work was suffering because of a recession, and he wanted to discuss the implications of becoming a 'house husband'.

> Jenny had been trained in teaching, but gave it up when she married. With two school-age children, she wanted to explore the possibilities of returning to work.

Consideration of the work–life balance may not initially be on the client's agenda in approaching a career counsellor, but may need to be addressed if, for example, the expression of a client's creativity at work is blocked, and there appears to be more opportunity to develop it outside work.

When a client has work–life balance issues, an underlying conflict of values often exists, as the following case study illustrates:

> Sandra came to career counselling saying that she was feeling 'burnt out' with social work, and tired and frustrated about all

the reorganisations and cuts made to the services in her local authority. Although she was presenting with the career need to assess alternative possibilities for the future, during the first meeting it emerged that she had just discovered she was pregnant. At the age of 40, she had recently become very close to a man with whom she worked, and they had begun a sexual relationship. Having been a determinedly successful 'career woman' all her working life, she was feeling very agitated and confused about this relationship, her pregnancy and the implications for her future. Sandra was feeling torn in two directions. One side of her desperately wanted to move in with her friend and have a child 'before it's too late'. The other side of her felt that to do this would mean abandoning her many work responsibilities and 'causes' and sinking into a cosy and stereotyped domesticity which would be a betrayal of much of what she had fought against all her working life.

For an in-depth discussion of career development issues for women, see Betz and Fitzgerald (1987).

Implications for career counsellors
The career counsellor needs to encourage the client to make a decision about the balance between work and the rest of life which is right for that individual at that particular time of his or her life. In order to be able to do this, career counsellors must be careful not to allow their own beliefs about male and female roles in relation to family and work to influence the career counselling. Clients who are in the process of making a significant change to the balance between work and the rest of their lives may require some support from the career counsellor over an extended period of time.

A knowledge of life stages and the issues which typically arise is useful when dealing with work–life balance issues, as is knowing about alternatives to full-time employment (see Chapter 7).

Discussion of work–life balance often uncovers unresolved personal issues, and the career counsellor should be sensitive to the potential need for referral for personal counselling.

Decision-making problems

'I can't decide what to do' is probably the most common presenting problem with which career counsellors are faced. It may simply be the case that a client lacks the occupational information on which to base a decision, but an inability to make a career decision is more likely to stem from other causes, as Derek's case study demonstrates:

> Derek was from Wales. He did exceptionally well at school, and went to Cambridge to read natural sciences. At first, although he felt out of place at times, he did very well. However, during his third year he became very unmotivated towards his studies, and this seemed to be connected with his lack of career direction. Exploration in several career counselling sessions revealed that Derek had never made a single educational decision himself, but had dutifully followed the advice of his teachers. In spite of his ability, he was also frightened of making a commitment to a particular career, in case it was the 'wrong' one and he failed.

Harren (1974) views self-concept and self-esteem as central to the ability to make a career decision. Self-concept refers to the degree of differentiation and integration the individual has been able to make. Self-esteem is the level of satisfaction with self.

Some clients present as not *knowing* who they are; we often hear the statement 'I don't know my strengths and weaknesses'. Lack of a well-differentiated self-concept may be 'normal' for an adolescent client's life stage, as adolescents are likely to be separating psychologically from their parents and developing an independent identity as an adult (Erikson, 1971). However, many adults who come for career counselling also lack a clear self-concept. These clients often ask for help in assessing their talents and capabilities in order that they can be better equipped to make a decision about which career direction to pursue. Other clients present as not *liking* who they are. They believe that they know themselves, but suffer from low self-esteem, and need help in increasing it.

Rational-emotive therapy has some useful frameworks to offer when considering career decision-making problems. Dryden (1979) states that, in his experience of career counselling, 'it is rare that a client is not subscribing to at least one of the irrational ideas outlined by Ellis [1962] that is relevant to his ability to make a career decision'. An example would be, 'It is absolutely essential for me to reach the top in my chosen career; if I don't it will be proof that I am a failure.'

Other decision-making problems that may be uncovered during career counselling include:

- pressures from third parties (most frequently parents or teachers) to follow a particular career direction;

- a conflict between two different parts of the self, for example the creative self and the conventional self. Such a conflict may reflect values introjected from parents (see Chapter 4);
- fear of taking risks: it is better to have the self-image of a person who has the potential to be a success than to take the risk of trying but failing and therefore having the self-image of a failure;
- not taking responsibility for making decisions: people constantly seek advice from others, and therefore always have a convenient scapegoat if the advice works out badly for them;
- a conflict between career needs and personal needs. Women are particularly subject to pressures to marry and start a family, but clients of either gender may face problems in making career decisions because of conflicts between home/family needs and career needs;
- fear of success operating simultaneously with a fear of failure, leading to paralysis.

Implications for career counsellors

The majority of clients who are finding difficulty in making a career decision because of lack of clarity about their strengths and weaknesses can be helped through self-assessment exercises and the use of psychometric tests and other instruments, as described in Chapters 4 and 5.

Often, just by identifying an irrational idea or an underlying conflict and becoming aware of it, the client will be able to come to a resolution (see Chapter 4 on overcoming blocks). Underlying conflicts can be brought to the surface and explored in more depth, perhaps using techniques such as those outlined in Chapter 5.

Individual decision-making styles vary, with some clients preferring a logical and systematic approach and others adopting a more intuitive, 'it feels right' style. Exercises which the career counsellor can offer the client to assist with decision making are described in Chapter 6.

Particularly in the case of a dependent client who wants the career counsellor to take responsibility for making a decision, the contracting stage needs to be clearly negotiated, and the client reminded of his or her responsibilities throughout the career counselling process.

A pattern of chronic indecisiveness which manifests itself not only in the arena of career decisions but throughout a client's life will require referral for personal counselling.

Problems in implementing a decision

> David had a PhD and had always seen his future career path
> in the academic world. However, there were very few vacan-
> cies, due to cutbacks in higher education, and he had made a
> number of applications for jobs, without success, over a
> period of two years.

Some clients come to career counselling with apparent clarity about
what they want to do. A choice has been made; the problem
presented is that for a number of possible reasons the choice
cannot be implemented. Some sociologists (for example Roberts,
1981) have argued that social structures such as the family, education system and community largely determine an individual's level
of educational attainment and aspiration. Together with economic
conditions and the state of the local labour market, most people
find themselves 'allocated' to a job, rather than 'choosing' a career
in any meaningful way.

Whatever the economic situation, it is inevitable that some
people apply for jobs or for training and are rejected, either
because they are unsuitable or because there is a limited number of
opportunities. In times of recession, many more people will
experience problems in implementing a career decision. It is helpful
to distinguish external from internal constraints. External
constraints are factors over which an individual has no control, for
example government economic policy, or the fact that certain jobs
are only to be found in specific locations. However, there is
inevitably some 'internal' reason why people come to career
counselling, otherwise they would modify their plans in the light of
external circumstances. Internal constraints cover factors in an
individual's personality, feelings or beliefs which act as a block to
their career development. Most commonly, when working with a
client, the career counsellor will encounter an interrelationship
between both sets of factors, as David's case study demonstrates:

> It emerged that David was feeling very angry and bitter
> towards a system which had, as he saw it, encouraged him to
> develop specialist skills and then had no use for them. The
> career counsellor encouraged him to express this frustration,
> and to think about the transferable skills which his research
> degree in a scientific subject gave him. David said that he had
> most enjoyed collecting and analysing data during his PhD
> studies. Testing confirmed an orientation towards data rather
> than people; David was actually not at all motivated towards
> the teaching element of the posts for which he had been

applying. He began to look at posts within the health service which required collecting and analysing medical statistics, and eventually found a job that suited him.

Other problems in implementing a career decision which may be encountered include:

- an unrealistic career aspiration;
- feelings of vulnerability due to previous experiences of rejection which lead a person to hold back from taking the risk of being rejected again;
- ineffective self-presentation, usually linked with poor self-esteem and/or lack of oral or written communication skills;
- discrimination (conscious or unconscious) in the employment market on the basis of age, gender, race, disability or social class;
- lack of financial resources to pursue appropriate training;
- the intervention of personal adversity in the form of an accident, illness, or a bereavement, for example;
- a 'career ceiling' may have been reached. This tends to be common in mid-life, where opportunities for advancement are limited;
- an unrealistic wish to find a quick and painless 'fix'. People may need support to accept that it takes time and effort to make changes happen.

Implications for career counsellors

Experiences of rejection often give rise to very powerful feelings which need to be explored in career counselling before progress can be made in developing a plan of action for the future. For example, unresolved grief about a previous rejection may complicate the process of coping with competitive recruitment procedures.

Problems in implementing a career decision arise frequently with people from 'minorities'. Some guidelines for the career counsellor in working with people who are at a disadvantage in the labour market because of, for example, their gender, racial or social class origins are given in Chapter 7. Clients who have experienced discrimination and want to consider legal redress may need referral for specialist legal help.

The practical and emotional implications of personal adversity (such as a bereavement or divorce) may need to be worked through before the individual is able to implement a career plan, and referral for personal counselling may be appropriate.

The external circumstances which appear to be blocking the

client should be explored. Some constraints are real, and the client will need to come to terms with them. Other 'external' constraints are more apparent than real, and may conceal an underlying internal conflict. Clients' apparent clarity about what they want to do should not be taken at face value. Sometimes clients who experience rejection are unconsciously 'sabotaging' themselves because they are ambivalent about their career choice, possibly because the career 'choice' was never actually their own.

Problems brought about by change in organisations

The kinds of change in an organisation that can cause people to come for career counselling (or be referred by their employer) include the following:

- reorganisation, leading to job loss/redundancy;
- a change in the nature of a job: for example primary teaching involves much more paperwork than it used to;
- technological changes, such as the impact of information technology on office jobs;
- change of boss: for example to a person whose philosophy and/or personal style is incompatible;
- change in organisational values: for example due to Health Service reforms, business acumen is valued more highly;
- the liquidation of a small business.

Redundancy

Although there is less stigma attached to redundancy in the recession-ridden 1990s, it is still rather an unmentionable word, often clothed in euphemistic phrases such as, 'The company has had to downsize', 'Your job has been deleted', or 'We'll have to let you go'. A person whose job has been made redundant may approach a career counsellor with a deep sense of shock, a feeling of shame, a reinforced impression of his or her own inadequacies, a strongly defiant reaction, or a sense of relief. Some people will actually say to the career counsellor: 'I have been made redundant', because they *feel* redundant. The reality is that usually it is the job, not the individual, which has been made redundant.

The process of movement from one life situation (for example employment) to another (for example unemployment) involves coming to terms with loss, and the intense feelings of grief experienced after a redundancy can be similar to those felt by the bereaved. The degree of pain felt will depend on many individual factors, but perhaps the length of time with the employer, expectancy of re-employment, previous unresolved experiences of loss and the available financial and emotional support are the key ones. The following case studies illustrate how the 'same' event (reorganisation and subsequent 'deletion' of a person's job) can be experienced quite differently because to these individual factors:

Timothy had been in the accounts department of his company for twenty-five years. He was proud of working for his company, and he worked 'beyond the call of duty'. Since his partner died of cancer two years previously, he had been working even longer hours. He was 49 years old, and had an ageing mother to support. When he heard his job was 'surplus to requirements' after a reorganisation, he was very upset. In career counselling, it took several meetings for Timothy to work through his feelings of shock, panic and grief.

Jan was 41. She had been employed in her job as a researcher for twelve years. However, although she liked doing research, she had ceased to enjoy working for her employing organisation. She had a new boss for whom she had very little respect, and for the past year she had been considering leaving. She had few financial commitments, and good emotional support at home. When she heard her job was 'deleted' due to financial cutbacks, her first reaction was a deep sense of relief. In career counselling, although she addressed some feelings of bitterness (that her boss appeared not to value her skills), she was able to come to terms with the emotional impact very rapidly.

Implications for career counsellors
Unless clients are willing to address their feelings, early pressure may be placed on the career counsellor to provide a solution which provides the best job match, and to give training in job-hunting techniques. It is important for the career counsellor to be vigilant to the degree to which clients' negative feelings are getting in the way of a rational consideration of their present situation and future plans.

In career counselling with clients who are experiencing change it is helpful to have an understanding of the process of transition. Adams et al. (1976) define a transition as 'a discontinuity in a person's life space'. Smith (1989) has suggested a 'transition curve', depicting stages of emotional 'adjustment' to change (see Figure 2.1). The 'stages' are not time bound, and they may recur.

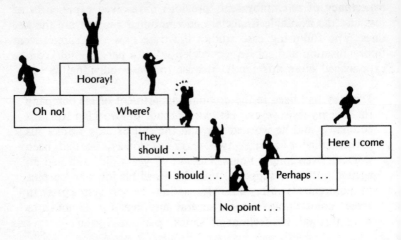

Figure 2.1 *The transition curve*
Source: Smith (1989)

Shock, denial:	Unable to believe that it has happened. 'You're joking!' A feeling of emptiness, perhaps numbness.
Euphoria:	Making the best of it, and minimising the reality of the change. 'Now I've got time to . . . paint the house, take a holiday . . . – I didn't like the job anyway.'
Pining:	Hoping that the job will come back – an unrealistic expectation that the next job will be exactly the same.
Anger:	Blaming someone – 'I never could work with him (my boss) anyway.' 'They should have . . .'
Guilt:	Self-blame – 'They chose me because I wasn't up to it/did something wrong.'
Apathy:	A sense of powerlessness and hopelessness as the reality sinks in.
Acceptance:	Letting go of the past, and the emergence of a new energy.

For someone deeply or mildly affected by change, the career counsellor will need to use the skills of counselling to allow the client sufficient time to 'work through' some of the above feelings. For very depressed clients, a referral may be in order.

It is helpful for career counsellors to have an understanding that the loss of a job can mean a good deal more than the loss of pay and a set of tasks, although these are of course important. Other 'losses' include self-esteem, a social outlet and a structure to the day.

Performance-related problems

> Clifford felt a failure in his job as a sales representative. His sales figures were consistently lower than those of his colleagues, and at his appraisal he was told that he 'lacked drive'.

Problems related to performance are perhaps the most obvious kind to precipitate the need for a visit to a career counsellor. 'Career' has, after all, been traditionally associated with achievement, and a career counsellor may well be seen as someone able to get the individual back on the, temporarily interrupted, path to success.

There are two ways in which performance-related problems may come to light. First, individuals may see themselves as having failed, or in a position where they might soon fail. Secondly, an employing organisation may have decided that an individual has, according to its requirements, failed. The two may or may not overlap. Box 2.3 lists some common presenting situations which may be linked to performance problems.

Box 2.3 *Some performance-related presenting problems*

- Dismissal
- Poor performance appraisal
- Failure to gain promotion after internal assessment
- Being 'passed over' for promotion in favour of a younger colleague
- Results consistently less good than those of colleagues
- Criticism from significant others (for example, parents, partners) for lack of achievement
- Continuing rejections on the job market
- 'Escaping' from failures by changing job/house/country
- Loss of motivation and effectiveness, which may arise because the person has reached a 'career plateau', perhaps through a lack of opportunities for career advancement.

At such times of perceived failure, feelings which may have lain dormant for years can surface. For example, a long-time low self-esteem led Paul to inappropriate career choices in the desire to gain recognition from his father, who was incapable of showing any love for his son because of his own 'stiff upper lip' upbringing. A perfectionist value led Alice (see p. 35) to accept from herself nothing but the best, even though she was performing very capably in most areas. As with redundancy, this 'sudden realisation' can come as a shock: 'I've never failed/had a poor assessment/been rejected before.'

Implications for career counsellors

As in the case of redundancy, the client's presenting feelings (for example depression, demoralisation, anger, shame, panic) need to be acknowledged and addressed to some extent at least before it is possible to establish the nature of the problem, which may involve:

- a mismatch between a person's capabilities and the current job's demands. This might have led to poor performance through the onset of stress. Such poor performance may have arisen through the job being overly or insufficiently demanding. For example, boredom from understimulation can lead to stress, which can lead to loss of motivation and effectiveness (see Mulligan, 1988);
- a person's promotion path being blocked in a large organisation owing to 'dead men's shoes', a slimming down of available promotional opportunities, or a poor relationship with a significant manager;
- a realistic deterioration of skills to keep up with the demands of the current job.

Where clients' performance standards are in question, it may be beneficial to give an aptitude test battery (see Chapter 5) in order to gain a relatively objective assessment of their strengths and weaknesses. Where personality factors affect job performance, personality questionnaires can be illuminating, as in Clifford's case:

Personality questionnaires revealed that Clifford was somewhat introverted, with a calm, even temperament and a thorough, patient approach to detail. Clifford recognised that he had been trying to succeed in an occupation for which he was temperamentally unsuited. He stopped trying to change himself, and instead changed his job from being a salesman to a 'behind the scenes' administrative support role.

The use of such tests and questionnaires must be undertaken with care – see Chapter 5 for a full discussion of their use in career counselling.

Relationship problems

It may seem strange for a career counsellor to be approached about a relationship problem. Indeed, this is often not the presenting problem, but may emerge in counselling as a significant consideration. In our practice, we specifically offer a service to assist clients to address relationship issues at work. It therefore becomes 'legitimate' for clients to bring these concerns up if they are at all aware that they exist. Justine's situation demonstrates how this can happen and markedly affect the direction of the career counselling.

> Justine was the director of a small company which had recently gone into liquidation. She approached career counselling ostensibly to 'check out' whether she was in the right career area. She had enjoyed her work, but her confidence had taken a knock. As the counselling progressed, she talked about how she tended to become over-involved with people at work. In particular, it was apparent that she had been depending too much on meeting her social needs through developing relationships with men with whom she worked closely. This led the career counsellor to work out with Justine, not the right occupation, but the best work environment to safeguard against this happening again, the kind of social activities she could take up outside employment and whether to take personal counselling to look more closely at her underlying needs.

Thus, the problem presented to the career counsellor led to exploration at a deeper level. It might have been appropriate to explore alternative occupations, but in Justine's case this seemed less important than to work out ways of decreasing her reliance on so many of her needs being met through work.

The kind of relationship problems brought to career counselling include:

- someone having a continuing abrasive work relationship, or set of relationships;
- a manager finding it hard to motivate staff;
- a mid-career client only able to progress by taking on managerial responsibility, but having no experience and little confidence to do so;

- an employee finding it hard to accept the authority of a particular manager;
- someone who finds it hard to deal effectively with *anyone* in authority;
- a person low in self-esteem finding it hard to take criticism;
- a subordinate disappointed with his or her boss for lack of guidance;
- someone experiencing an unusually strong sense of competition with peers, perhaps expressed through 'put-downs' at meetings.

Implications for career counsellors

Relationship problems may not necessarily be the ones clients state early on in career counselling as issues they want to address. The contract initially agreed with the client may either have to be sufficiently broad, or be redefined as appropriate.

Career counsellors helping clients to deal with relationship problems can adopt a number of strategies. The use of personality and other questionnaires dealing with personal style may help clients to identify and 'own' their particular traits and style. Skills training, such as assertion and dealing with meetings through rehearsal and practice, may be possible within a career counselling contract, or a referral may be suggested.

It is useful for career counsellors to appreciate some of the underlying issues associated with relationships at work, in particular, how people may recreate their relationships with parents or other significant figures with people at work. For example, a client who is disappointed with the lack of guidance he has received from his parents may express disappointment with his boss for lack of guidance. It may be possible to allow clients to see how their behaviour is linked in this way. For further exploration, a referral for personal counselling might be in order.

Expression and repression of creativity

What happens to the creativity encouraged in primary school, but discouraged from the age of 14 upwards except for the most talented? For example, those young people not taking art beyond the age of 14 may grow up believing that, since they are not apparently artistic, they are not creative. This is not the case, as it is possible to express creativity by, for example, innovation and development of an idea, project or product. Of course, this might take place in or out of work, or both.

The 'Protestant work ethic' is very strong, and many people

see work as a very serious business, incompatible with the 'fun' element necessary in creativity. Creativity issues often emerge during mid-life. We often see clients who have so devoted themselves to doing well at work that they sacrifice the expression of their creativity in all parts of their lives. Alice's example, below, demonstrates how she sacrificed her creativity to please her father.

Alice had worked for eight years in an accountancy firm. She had been successful, but the effects of stress had caused her to take time off. Through career counselling, she realised that she had been striving so hard for success to please her father, who had thoroughly approved of her promotions and increasing salary. Alice subsequently decided to seek work where she could combine her successful 'organised' self with her creative 'arty' side. Career counselling enabled her to realise the importance to her of this 'repressed' creativity, and also that she did not have to give up completely her organised self as well.

Implications for career counsellors
Clients who present to career counsellors as feeling bored, dull, grey and flat *may* be suffering from repressed creativity, the very part of them which represents vitality and energy. Somehow it has been suppressed, sapped or diverted. For those clients who are not able to realise, either partly or fully, their creativity through their work, it may be feasible to develop or revive a creative hobby outside employment.

The use of personality questionnaires and self-assessment exercises can be useful in highlighting clients' needs for expressing their creativity. The data produced from such exercises can give clients the confidence to 'do something about it'.

For people who want to express their creativity in their career, Dail (1989) is a helpful workbook, making use of imagery and fantasy techniques.

Summary

In this chapter we have discussed the problems that clients bring to career counselling, in the belief that it can help career counsellors to show empathy and understanding if they can quickly recognise the common questions and dilemmas faced by people. However, we consider that it is important not to use this recognition to 'sum up' or pigeonhole the client, thereby confusing the general *problem* with the individual *person*.

The problems clients bring and the underlying issues have been illustrated with case studies which give the flavour of career counselling in practice. The next four chapters examine the career counselling process in detail. Chapter 3 looks at the initial stages of screening, contracting and early exploration of the client's presenting problem.

3
Screening, Contracting and Exploring

It is important for the career counsellor to be concerned with what happens *before* the first counselling meeting because it can have a profound effect on the career counselling relationship. The stages of screening and contracting are actually part of constructing a relationship with any client, and have particular relevance to the role and expectations of a *career* counsellor.

Screening is a process which usually occurs before the counsellor and client contract to meet. It enables the counsellor to gather information about the prospective client, and the client to gain information about the counsellor and the service provided. Such information can assist both to decide whether to proceed further.

Contracting is a process by which counsellor and client come to a clear understanding about working methods and their respective roles in the career counselling. Sometimes screening may take place during the initial contracting phase, as the counsellor and client may, as yet, be less than fully committed.

As we made clear in the introductory chapter, in career counselling the responsibility for decision making is with the client. Clients may not, however, be prepared or ready to undertake this responsibility. There may be a continuing expectation that the career counsellor should be able to guide the client into the 'right' career. It is therefore important to contract with people to ensure maximum readiness to work with a counselling, rather than an advice, approach. People may not necessarily prefer an advisory approach; they may simply not know that 'counselling' can be effective – so the screening and contracting stages of the career counselling process are in themselves educative.

Screening and contracting are of course inextricably linked. By responding to statements of what career counselling can and cannot do, clients can make an informed decision whether to contract in or out.

This chapter addresses considerations about structuring a career counselling service, and how potential clients can be encouraged to approach career counselling in an active, as opposed to a passive, state of mind. The nature of clients' expectations are discussed.

The contracting that takes place face to face in the first meeting during the exploration of the client's presenting problem and throughout the career counselling process is subsequently tackled.

Screening

Screening in writing

A well-written leaflet for prospective clients will help to minimise misunderstandings about what a career counselling service can offer. A prospectus, leaflet or brochure has a number of purposes:

Educative Prospective users of a service may not know of this kind of approach to career counselling. Writing down what is expected of clients sets out what the contract involves and educates at one and the same time. Those people who feel uncertain whether they can comply with these expectations can choose to ask further questions, either on the telephone or in person (see following sections). This can help to clarify their thinking and perhaps increase trust in what may be an unfamiliar process.

Contractual By stating what the service can and cannot do, and what is expected of clients, the terms of an offer are being set out. Having a written document increases the chances that a client will have 'taken in' what the contract means. This is preferable to leaving matters open to the vagaries of telephone discussions, referrals and recommendations.

Information giving Written information can and should reflect accurately the services offered. It should include details of the nature of the service, the qualifications of the counsellors, and details of any other facilities, such as libraries, referral resources and job-hunting training.

Trust building Stating clearly what is on offer reduces any opportunity for unrealistic expectations. Written information can create a certain 'image' of a service which, hopefully, is comprehensive, caring and professional. This in itself lays the foundations for building trust.

Screening on the telephone

A telephone conversation is more personal than a piece of paper. Voice contact can do much to build up (or undermine) trust. Adequate time and personnel resources are necessary in order to operate telephone screening effectively.

Questions can be dealt with more individually prior to commitment to any meeting. Information which might be useful should the person choose to become a client can be revealed:

1 The source of the referral, and consequent expectations (for example, 'You saw my friend/son/partner and were very helpful').
2 The urgency of the situation (for example, 'I have to apply to courses within a month').
3 The inquirer's initial perception of what a career counselling service can offer (for example, 'I've been working abroad for five years and have no idea how to approach the UK job market').

In telephone screening it is possible to give and receive feedback and fulfil the educative, contracting and, particularly, the trust-building functions of screening mentioned already. Information can of course be given, but this may be more easily absorbed in written form. A subsequent discussion, either on the telephone or in person, can reinforce and expand on the information given in writing and deal with further questions.

Screening in person
Face-to-face introductory meetings with a number of potential clients facilitated by a counsellor are an effective way of increasing the realism of expectations. This does not require commitment on either side. Such meetings are (a) economical – you can say the same words to several prospective clients at the same time; (b) more 'personal' than written or telephone communications; and (c) real – they show that you exist, who you are and what the place is like physically.

At our 'open meetings', people often start off by saying they are looking for advice, or that they want to be 'put on the right path'. These may be the socially acceptable words to use – it is harder to ask directly for help or for something less tangible and obvious, such as 'someone to listen to me'. It may also be easier to justify the time and money to interested third parties if you end up with a tangible written report or even a new career! One of the aims of the open meeting is to put over the service as one offering counselling and not advice, to encourage clients to take an active, rather than passive, approach.

We find that clients who come to open meetings are better informed about what the process entails, and about their role and responsibility as a client. If they decide to proceed, they are better prepared psychologically for career counselling. In addition, they have dealt with many of the little questions that are often of concern – such as, 'How do I get there?' or 'Where do I park?' – by practical experience. Clients are therefore likely to be less nervous and uncertain about what the place will be like when they arrive.

Perhaps because of this initial work, we have found that the trust level is higher at the beginning of the counselling than with clients who have only received written information.

Open meetings can also give useful information to the counsellor. For example:

- Has the person had current or past experience of psychotherapy or counselling?
- What has been the person's experience of any previous career help?
- What are the person's experiences and expectations of tests?
- What is the person's level of pain or distress, and readiness for career counselling?

The last point raises the question of whether and how to discourage people who are unlikely to benefit from the career counselling process, and what kind of referral resources are available. Usually people screen themselves out. Occasionally, however, we have to discourage people. We would always try to suggest an alternative source of help if a personal issue seemed to be more prominent than the career problem, or if the counsellor judged the client's expectations to be too unrealistic to work with.

Written preparation by client
Some kind of written preparation by clients is another way of encouraging a more active approach to the career counselling process. It can also enable them, before the first meeting, to decide to screen themselves out, and is a test of their commitment. We ask clients to complete a 'background questionnaire', and to write briefly about their perceived strengths and weaknesses. A few suggestions of appropriate questions or issues to ask clients to write about are given in Box 3.1.

There is a big difference between clients who have and have not completed some written work prior to the first meeting. As one ex-client said: 'The introductory homework can only be done with thought – you put yourself at a disadvantage without doing the preparation. You don't arrive at the first meeting with a completely

---

Box 3.1   *Suggestions for written preparation*

- Biodata (name, address, telephone, age, marital status, etc.)
- Education and career details
- Aspects of education, training and career enjoyed/disliked
- Aspects of education and training good/poor at
- Details of non-career achievements
- Occupations of family, partner
- Occupations considered
- Hobbies and interests
- Self-assessment of strengths and weaknesses in career
- Description of current situation
- What kind of help is sought from the career counselling

---

blank mind, expecting to be led by the hand through the process. You have done some pretty hard reflection.'

Contracting

The question of money: who pays and for what?
If the career counsellor works for an independent, fee-paying service, the question of money arises. Clients either pay for themselves, or are sponsored by an interested third party, perhaps a parent or employer.

When a client pays a fee, this may affect his or her expectations of 'value'. Value may be seen in terms of a tangible end-product, an 'after' state which can be shown to others as having been influenced by the counselling. But clients do not just commit themselves financially. They give time (a good deal of it for many of our clients), both during and between meetings, and a willingness to participate actively in, rather than just passively 'attend', career counselling.

The issue of money is significant. It probably encourages the client to take contracting prior to commitment more seriously. The questions being addressed include:

What will I be getting for my money? Will it be worth it?
How will I justify the expenditure, given my other commitments?
Can I and do I want to afford this now?

Where possible, we do encourage clients who are earning, and who are over the age of 18, to pay at least a proportion of the fees themselves. This increases, though never guarantees, the likelihood of commitment.

If an interested third party is paying, there may be an extra expectation which needs to be addressed, or at least acknowledged. With all clients, but particularly in the case of third-party referrals, the question of confidentiality must be addressed.

Confidentiality and third-party referrals

As in any counselling, it is assumed that confidentiality will be offered and maintained by the counsellor and any staff who have access to client files. The *Code of Ethics and Practice for Counsellors* (British Association for Counselling, 1990) describes confidentiality as 'a means of providing the client with safety and privacy . . . any limitation on the degree of confidentiality offered is likely to diminish the usefulness of counselling'. One way round this dilemma is to allow the third party some 'time', probably on the telephone, to air any thoughts and feelings, whilst being clear that nothing will be revealed of the content of the counselling itself. This gives respect to someone who is usually concerned for and caring of the client, whilst maintaining the contract of confidentiality. In career counselling, particular pressures can be placed on this contract of confidentiality from third parties, who may expect to receive feedback from the career counsellor.

With employers, we think it is reasonable for some 'return' to be expected for the money invested. Most employers do seem content to leave any feedback about the career counselling in the hands of the employee. We always make it clear to both parties that the counsellor will not give any feedback direct to the employer concerning the content of the counselling. The 'return' the employer can expect comes in the form of employees who are more clear about their strengths, weaknesses and career direction, and who are more motivated. In our experience, employees who have been through career counselling are happy to share much, if not all, of the content with their employers, when any apparent threat has been removed and a positive plan agreed. The following case study indicates how clear contracting with both the employer and the client led to a worthwhile outcome.

Bernard had been passed over for promotion, his management ability having recently been severely criticised. He had, however, refused to accept this adverse 'diagnosis' by his employer. They had reached a stalemate, and a referral for career counselling was suggested by a colleague in the same organisation, so that Bernard could gain an objective and independent view of his skills and potential.

Although the organisation had used the career counselling service over many years, this was the first referral by Bernard's manager. After the initial telephone contact, and a subsequent letter, it became clear that he expected a report to be written on Bernard after one interview! A subsequent telephone discussion led to an agreement which was clarified in writing. It was agreed that: (a) there would be four or five meetings; (b) there would be no feedback by the counsellor on the content of the discussions; (c) following the career counselling, Bernard would be expected to debrief his manager, but would have control over the content discussed.

In the first meeting, the confidentiality contract was restated to Bernard, who initially found it hard to trust. Through the establishment of a good rapport, however, Bernard was able to assess himself in a non-threatening atmosphere. By the end of the career counselling, he decided that he was more suited to an administrative, rather than a staff management, role. A few weeks later, a letter was received from Bernard's manager expressing how pleased he was with both the process and the outcome.

One reason why it is so important to insist on confidentiality is because of the danger that career counselling can be seen by the employer as a way of gathering external feedback to confirm a previously held view that, for example, the employee is not suited to a particular position. In such a potentially threatening referral situation, it will be hard, if not impossible, to establish the trust necessary for open and effective career counselling.

With parents who are paying, the situation is somewhat different. Parents who pay for their son's or daughter's career counselling may press the career counsellor for information, or to produce a particular result. Although, through screening and contracting, it can be made clear that nothing will be revealed outside of the counselling relationship without the client's prior permission, pressure can subtly be brought to bear. The following comments are typical of those we have heard:

We are paying and expect some kind of written report.
We only want the best for Johnny, and he won't tell us anything.
How's the counselling going?

Why aren't you making any suggestions to Johnny? He doesn't seem any further forward.
Really, why are you suggesting this career to Johnny? [You never did!]
We know him, and he'd just be out of his depth.

Such comments can seduce the unwary career counsellor into revealing confidences.

We always try to ensure that young people make their own appointments and have read our literature. This, however, is not always possible, and particular attention must be paid to explaining in the first meeting what the career counselling process involves and what is expected from the client. If this is not done, there is a danger that a client's lack of commitment could well manifest itself in non-attendance and last-minute cancellations.

Occasionally, a parent will ring up, and express a concern about how the counselling is proceeding. We are usually happy to offer a little time to concerned parents, being clear that it is the parent who then becomes the client. Listening skills can be used and counselling support given, but the content of the daughter's or son's career counselling will not be revealed. There has been one occasion when a parent, fully respecting the confidentiality contract and recognising his own needs, booked a session for himself! The following example demonstrates how we responded to a concerned parent, for the benefit of everyone concerned.

Helena was 22 years old and had worked with animals since she left school, but wanted a change as there were no further prospects. Her father (Mr Vaughan) had obtained a brochure and phoned up to book her in for career counselling. The member of staff who took his call explained how the service operated, and suggested that his daughter read the brochure and then book the appointments herself.

At the contracting stage, it was clear that Helena was there for herself and committed to the counselling process. The counsellor enquired about Helena's relationship with her father. Helena said that he had always been very supportive and although he was paying for the sessions, he wasn't pushing her in a particular direction. The counsellor also clarified the confidentiality agreement, and made it clear that Helena (and not the counsellor) was responsible for giving any feedback to her father.

As the career counselling progressed, Helena's lack of knowledge of the world of work became apparent, and the counsellor explained that Helena could use the careers library to inform herself about various possible career options. Helena set off with enthusiasm to find out more about careers.

Before the final meeting was scheduled, Mr Vaughan phoned up and spoke to a member of the support staff. Sounding very anxious, he said that his daughter needed her horizons broadened because she had been working in such a limited field, and he wanted the counsellor to give Helena a range of suggestions of suitable careers. The member of staff listened, and then explained to Mr Vaughan that although clients are responsible for generating their own ideas, there are careers information resources to help them in the process.

At Helena's final meeting, she was not ready to make a final decision about her choice of career, but drew up a shortlist of careers to investigate in more detail. At the end of the session, the counsellor asked Helena how she would be giving feedback to her father, and Helena said she had arranged to have lunch with him. She said she thought he would be pleased because even though she had not reached a final decision, her horizons were now much broader!

Here, we see that, by using a trained member of staff (*not* the counsellor) to talk to the parent, the counsellor was not pressured in any direct way to defend the approach offered. In this situation, as in many others, the parent may have been using the career counselling to give his daughter the kind of attention he would like to have given her himself, but could not. The telephone call was one way of reassuring himself that this was happening.

Screening and contracting in the first meeting
However much information a client may have had beforehand, the first meeting with the career counsellor is the time to establish and confirm the contract with the client. If someone else has been involved in arranging career counselling on a client's behalf, this is the time to test out the client's own commitment to the process.

From reading any written preparation, and during the first meeting, the counsellor can glean a good deal about the client's commitment. It may also be possible, through discussion and appropriate questioning, to discover any destructive patterns of behaviour which the client may be bringing into the counselling relationship. For example, a client who has a feeling of constantly being let down may unconsciously 'sabotage' the career counselling.

Essentially, we are asking ourselves whether this is the right place, at the right time, and with the right counsellor – for this client. A difficulty may arise when it is clear that there are personal issues which need addressing before a career decision can be made. It may be that all a client can bear to admit to at the time is the career issue, and the need for counselling is expressed as a desire for career counselling (that is, *not* ongoing personal counselling or psychotherapy). 'Going for career counselling' sounds more socially acceptable than 'going for therapy'. It has a clear structure and aim which clients can talk about more easily with their partner, family or friends. Once they have arrived in the career counselling room, clients may want to use some of the counselling time for discussing deeper issues. After all, what is 'career' or 'employment' other than what people choose to *be* for a good proportion of their lives, particularly in terms of achievement, success, recognition and the attainment of compatible values?

A crucial consideration in the contracting stage is that, although we are contracting with clients about objectives which are to do with the career 'externals' (for example, 'Should I stay with or leave medicine?'), we are aware at the same time of possible internal agendas concerning thoughts and feelings (for example, 'I have decided to leave medicine – I want support during this "letting go" phase'). Such issues raise the question of the boundary between career and personal counselling.

Boundaries between career and personal counselling

As career counsellors, we are offering a range of possible services, as listed in Box 1.1 (p. 7). We are not offering long-term or ongoing personal counselling contracts.

We are aiming to establish a collaborative or Adult-to-Adult relationship, not a Parent–Child one (to use Transactional Analysis terms; see Stewart, 1989). We find it helpful to liken the career counselling process to a journey. For example: 'This is where you are now. There's a place that you might want to get to; in between there is a journey. Our meetings are only part of your journey. Very few people get to their destination by the last meeting here. But you should travel some way down the road.' This gives licence to the client to accept the career counselling as a process, and feel less obliged to seek an answer by the final meeting. It also encourages clients to take responsibility for making their journey a productive one, and therefore to be fully motivated to complete 'homework' assignments (see Chapter 5).

However effective a screening process has been, very occasionally a person whose degree of distress is so strong that this collaborative, Adult-to-Adult career counselling is unlikely to be effective will 'slip through the net' and arrive for a first meeting. As in any form of counselling, the decision about whether or not to take on a client for career counselling must be based on ethical considerations, the level of rapport (although this of course can change) and the counsellor's professional judgement about whether the counselling will be of value to this client *now*. Referral may be required. As most counsellors realise, making a referral is a delicate skill, and can always be perceived at some level as a rejection.

If a client is in psychotherapy, does the psychotherapist know that the client is having career counselling? If not, why not, and what are the implications? Could the career counsellor be misused as an alternative therapist? We advise clients to let their therapist know they are attending career counselling. Again, this helps to set the boundaries of the counselling. One advantage of working with clients familiar with counselling or psychotherapy is their awareness of the 'counselling' (not advice) nature of the contract. A disadvantage is that they can easily slip into 'therapy mode'. This can be minimised by reminding the client, when appropriate, of the *career* aspect of the counselling contract.

Number, length and frequency of meetings
Whatever way the career counselling is structured, it is important that clients are briefed accordingly. This is always true, but perhaps especially so in the case of single consultations, where clients may expect to be given advice on the best career. Briefing can be in the form of a concise note which reflects, in tone and content, the nature of the service offered and the contribution expected of both the counsellor and client.

Number of meetings Flexibility is vital, fitting the service provided to the needs of the client, rather than the reverse. However, we have found that a programme of four or five meetings is about right for the majority of people.

If tests are administered, meetings can be structured as follows:

- *1st visit:* contracting, exploring (1½–2 hours);
- *2nd visit:* testing (2–6 hours);
- *3rd visit:* feedback and discussion of homework assignments and test results (1½–2 hours);
- *4th visit:* discussion of reflections on previous meeting; occupational/educational information (1–1½ hours);
- *5th visit:* action planning; coaching in job-hunting techniques (1–1½ hours).

If tests or questionnaires are not used, fewer meetings may be needed. In either case, it is useful to contract for a specified number of meetings: having an end-point in sight can sometimes galvanise a client into a ready state for 'moving on to the next stage', which might, for example, be a preparedness to carry out research into one or two careers. Career counsellors should also be prepared to renegotiate the number and timing of meetings, particularly if a personal issue emerges in the process of counselling which requires further time, a different emphasis or a possible referral.

The frequency of meetings may, but should not necessarily, be influenced by the urgency with which clients need to make a career decision (frequency of meetings may also be affected by more mundane factors, such as the distance the client has to travel). A gap of at least three or four days between meetings allows time for reflection and the completion of homework assigments. The gap may be longer later in the career counselling process, as the client may need to progress with some practical research before returning for a 'review' meeting (see Chapter 6).

Single consultations   A single consultation can be of benefit if the client has a fairly clear self-concept and a reasonable level of self-esteem and, prior to the meeting, undertakes some written preparation. Some clients will need little more than a single discussion on setting career goals, the strategy of job hunting or where and how to find relevant occupational information. Other occasions when a single consultation may suffice or be preferable include situations where:

- the client is on the brink of a decision, and wants a single meeting to clarify his or her thinking;
- the client wants to access careers information – a single meeting might help to gain the confidence needed to do so;
- time is at a premium. A single meeting, together with written preparation, may help give some structure to thoughts, feelings and ideas.

In most cases, however, we believe that much more can be gained from a series of counselling meetings, combined with the use of various tests, questionnaires and self-assessment exercises.

Setting objectives at the contracting stage
Establishing some objectives provides structure for both the client and the counsellor, and can be a basis for a subsequent review of

progress. Any objectives set should not become a straitjacket, but should merely provide a general framework for the counselling. Getting a client to say something like, 'I want to be more clear about my career strengths and weaknesses', encourages ownership, an emphasis on process, and a career focus. A more specific objective might be, 'I want to understand why I can't hold down a job for more than six months', or, 'I want to decide between moving to a generalist management role or remaining within my specialism.'

Typical client objectives are listed in Box 3.2.

Box 3.2 *Objectives for career counselling*

- I want to decide on my next career step.
- I want to decide whether to change career or employer.
- I want to improve my job-hunting techniques and maintain self-esteem while I am unemployed.
- I want to develop strategies for coping with relationships at work.
- I want to decide whether or not to return to full-time education.
- I want to increase my awareness and knowledge of the requirements for success in several occupations.
- I want to consider my suitability for self-employment.
- I want to develop an outline career plan for the next five years.
- I want to decide whether to continue to tertiary education, to train via employment or have a 'gap year'.

Some clients are less concerned to make a career *decision* ('Should I follow path x or y?') than to have support to deal with a career-related issue. This may be about coming to terms with a loss, such as redundancy, not being promoted, coping with a new boss, or the increased financial pressure of a spouse/partner re-entering education.

It is also possible that the client's initial objectives are misguided in some way, and here, too, the counsellor should remain flexible enough to alter the contract appropriately, as the following case study demonstrates.

George had been a moderately successful musician. But, over the past few years, his engagements had been reduced to the point where he had to take on alternative employment. Through his girlfriend, he had obtained work as a 'librarian/researcher' for a photographic agency. He approached career counselling, attended an open meeting, and booked in for a series of sessions. In his written preparation, he expressed a desire to be told exactly of the openings available in his field. He enjoyed, and was praised for, his work, and wanted to continue in this direction, but could see no future or security in his present employment. With a steady relationship, and a currently stable income, he wanted to build for the future. It soon became clear that his expectations of career counselling were unrealistic and, since he knew what he wanted to do, there were other issues to address. He knew little about training opportunities in librarianship or information work and felt very unsure about how to approach job hunting. The counsellor redefined the contract to this end, giving him access to appropriate information, helping him to develop an appropriate CV and providing interview practice.

In this instance it became necessary for the career counsellor to combine counselling skills with information-giving and even teaching, demonstrating and coaching skills.

The influence of tests on client expectations
Client perceptions about psychometric testing need to be explored during contracting. Many people are aware that psychometric tests are used to assess people for jobs. They may also be aware of their usage in vocational guidance, where a 'test and tell' approach is adopted – the client is 'assessed' and a short interview provides a basis for the consultant, usually an occupational psychologist, to advise on careers commensurate with the test results.

In counselling, it is vital that any use of psychometric tests and other questionnaires should serve, rather than dominate, the counselling relationship. Test 'results' can be used as a basis for discussion, the evaluation of self-perceptions and a way of addressing feelings concerning performance. At best, such results are only a guide, and any written or face-to-face screening and contracting should emphasise this fact. Clients may need to be reminded that tests will not be used to 'select' them for a particular occupation. This can help to remove any potential confusion between this *counselling* meeting and previous *selection* interviews.

Another consideration when contracting is that the client may be affected by feelings about past tests, examinations and other performance-related experiences. If the influence of these feelings is very strong, it may be wise to leave out any testing altogether, or at least until a later meeting, when a greater level of safety has been established with the client. See Chapter 5 for a fuller discussion on the use of tests and questionnaires in career counselling.

Exploration

The process of contracting already described is inextricably linked with the process of exploration. During the first meeting, it helps if the counsellor bears the following tasks in mind:

- building rapport to enable the client to discuss their concerns freely;
- helping the client to explore what and who has influenced career and educational choices;
- exploring any written preparation undertaken by the client.

Building rapport

As in any counselling relationship, there is a great deal which can be done to build rapport and trust quickly, and enable clients to talk freely. This may, to some extent, have been done through the earlier contracting, particularly if the client has been to an introductory meeting. However, most clients tend to arrive feeling fairly nervous and uncertain of what will happen. The counsellor's job at this stage is largely to enable clients to talk as easily as possible about themselves.

The *physical setting* is important. It will help if the 'tone' of the office is friendly, the chairs of similar type and with no barriers, such as a desk, between counsellor and client. If it is specifically career counselling which is being offered, a few work-related magazines on a small table might be useful if clients are kept waiting.

It may be helpful (for the counsellor) and interesting (for the client) to hang some quotation on the wall which encapsulates some aspect of the philosophy of career counselling. Ours is:

> I can help you plan your route
> draw maps
> but not act as your tourist guide

Career counselling requires all the basic counselling skills of listening, responding with respect and empathy, asking open questions and summarising, which have been well documented elsewhere (Egan, 1990; Inskipp, 1988). Allowing the client to tell his or her 'story' will in itself increase rapport. An open question to begin the meeting, such as 'What made you decide on career counselling at this point in your life?', will usually encourage the client to talk freely. In addition, it is possible to pick up some information which may be useful later in the career counselling. Box 3.3 suggests a number of questions for first meetings.

Box 3.3 *Suggested questions for first meeting*

Issue	Question
Was the client personally recommended?	How did you hear of us? Why did you choose this service?
What are the client's expectations?	What do you hope to gain from career counselling?
How is the counselling valued by the client? Are there any third-party expectations?	What made you decide on career counselling at this point in your life? (a useful opening question)
Has the client received any previous career help?	What kind of career help have you had in the past? [for example] At the age of 13 did you have any help in choosing options? Who influenced your choices? (Ditto for other choice points)
What is the general emotional state of the client? Is 'career' the presenting problem?	What issues are going on in your life at the moment? What else is happening?
Is client receiving psychotherapy or other support?	What supports do you have at the moment?
What are the client's expectations of testing?	How do you expect tests might be able to help?

Exploring influences on career and educational choices
Exploring how the client has made career decisions in the past at major choice points (selecting options at school; decision about first job; decisions about changing jobs) can assist the career

counsellor in formulating hunches about the degree to which the client has taken responsibility for decision making and follow-through in the past.

Kathy came to career counselling because her first year as an accountancy trainee had been a miserable one, and she had been confused about her career direction for some time. Her teachers had told her what subjects to study, and her parents had told her to take a degree in business studies because she would be able to get a good job. At college, all her friends went on to study accountancy, so Kathy followed suit. She had never taken responsibility for a single career decision.

Exploring any early ideas the client may have had as a child or adolescent and what happened to them can be helpful at this stage. Unfulfilled career ideas or special interests might still be resurrected in some form. The client may need to explore feelings (possibly of loss) associated with unfulfilled dreams, as the following case study shows:

At the first career counselling meeting Alex appeared depressed and flat. The question 'What did you want to do when you grew up?' revealed that he loved drawing and painting as a child, but in secondary school he was told that his art was not good enough to make a success of it commercially. A flood of emotion poured out. He was near to tears as he confessed that he had never drawn or painted since, and expressed bitter resentment about the advice he had been given to train in banking instead. Several meetings later, Alex reported that he had enrolled on an evening class in art.

Exploring written preparation
The first meeting is also the appropriate time to go through the client's written preparation, over which he or she may have taken considerable trouble. Clients will often signpost their difficulties very clearly in the written preparation. This usually signals readiness to explore the topic:

Under the section on health in her preparation questionnaire, Heather wrote 'severe arthritis'. During the first meeting, it emerged that she had been a successful (and happy) nursery nurse, but she was unable to continue to work with children because of the disabling effects of arthritis in her hands. Subsequent counselling focused on her feelings of frustration and loss. This was a necessary stage in a process of 'letting go' in preparation for changing direction.

Some clients are, quite naturally, more reticent about exposing very personal information in writing before they have met the counsellor, and rapport will need to be good before such information is divulged:

> Although he did not mention it in his written preparation, Danny had been supporting his partner, who eventually died of AIDS. Through their contact with AIDS counsellors, Danny became interested in counselling as a career, and wanted to assess his suitability for it.

Sometimes helpful information can emerge from exploring any gaps or discrepancies in the information presented:

> The counsellor noticed that Michael had missed out a whole year of his life in his 'background questionnaire'. Exploration of this gap revealed that he had been asked to leave after the first year of a course at agricultural college, and brought out his acute feelings of embarrassment about failing in his father's eyes (he came from a long line of farmers).

Using the clues raised by clients' behaviour

An important counselling skill is to take note of any ways in which clients reproduce in their career counselling the very emotions, attitudes and behaviour that they are finding difficulty with in their lives. Clients often give hints about these issues, not through what they say directly, but in a very vivid manner through the way they behave.

Being able to establish the nature and source of the initial referral can be an invaluable source of information about the client's issues and their relationship to career counselling. Did they hear of you from someone yesterday, and want a meeting tomorrow? Or did they ring up, request a brochure, and sit on it for a year before making an appointment, which they then cancel at the last minute, before booking again? Were they recommended? If so, by whom? By an ex-client who said the career counselling 'changed his life'? Or by a counsellor, psychotherapist or GP? Did they find you on a listing or in the telephone directory? Have they researched several counselling services in a thorough and systematic way? Clients also show something of their personalities and problems through the way they make appointments. Are they quick and businesslike? Or tentative and long-winded? The following case study demonstrates how the manner in which the meetings were arranged gave the career counsellor some important clues concerning Tina's problem:

> The brother of this client originally booked in himself for career counselling. Ten days before his initial appointment, he telephoned to say that both he and his sister Tina would like to attend an open meeting. He said he was uncertain if he needed the career counselling, but his sister might. At the open meeting, he made it clear he would like to 'hand over' his appointments lock, stock and barrel to his sister. 'Don't worry,' he said, 'I can give her all the preparation forms.' He hardly allowed her to speak at all in making the arrangements for *her* meetings! The counsellor making the appointments made sure that she received a brochure of her own, new preparation papers and a fresh letter of confirmation.

In the counselling meetings, it turned out that the issue of 'independence vs conformity' was a crucial one for her, as was the matter of being able to achieve her power as a woman! Tina expected to be 'told' of the best career solution (she was used to authority figures making decisions for her), until it was established in the first meeting that she could use the career counselling service as a way of discovering herself, as her counsellor had no vested interest in persuading her to move in a particular direction.

Another useful pointer is the counsellor's own feelings towards the client:

> Kathy's counsellor found at the first meeting that she was strongly tempted to respond in a maternal fashion towards Kathy. These feelings were unusual for this counsellor, and her hunch that one of the important issues to be tackled in the counselling was Kathy's dependency needs and her avoidance of taking responsibility for making her own decisions turned out to be accurate.

The counsellor's feelings should act as no more than the basis of a hunch or hypothesis to be later checked out. Such feelings may reflect something in the counsellor, rather than in the client.

The whole-person approach

As we have seen, clients can bring one or several issues to career counselling. There is potential for confusion between personal and career counselling, not least because there can be a very real connection between the two. In the following case it would have been impossible and unproductive to attempt to explore career issues without considering the context of the client's life as a whole:

> Nina was from Cyprus, and nearing the end of a second degree course when she came for career counselling. She was being pressurised by her family to marry a particular man, about whom she had strong doubts; she liked him as a friend but did not see him as a potential husband. In the first meeting, it emerged that she had been continuing with her studies as a way of avoiding making difficult decisions, concerning career and marriage. Now that her time as an 'academic' was coming to an end, she had no choice but to address these decisions.

The career counsellor needs flexibility to move back and forth between all matters of concern to a client, whilst recognising that the central focus is career issues. If personal issues threaten to overwhelm the career counselling process, a referral for personal counselling may be necessary.

Summary

Effective screening and contracting lay a sound foundation for subsequent career counselling. The career counsellor needs to be alert from the point of first contact to issues which, if left unresolved, may have the power to sabotage the whole process.

The kind of contracting which is necessary will depend on a number of considerations, including clients' readiness for career counselling and their experience of counselling as a process. There is inevitably a different starting point for each individual. Once counselling has begun, however, it is necessary to keep a careful watch on clients' commitment, and whether the contract needs readdressing. Contracting is like a thread running through the whole career counselling process.

We have also discussed the structure of first meetings and important topics for the client to explore. During this phase, clients will begin to clarify their interests, skills and values. The counsellor will need to be alert to underlying themes and be aware of hunches or hypotheses about the client, the problem and any likely outcomes, as these may be helpful to pursue at the next stage of the career counselling process.

In the following two chapters, the next stage is discussed:

enabling clients to develop a clearer understanding of themselves in relation to the world of work. This is the heart of the career counselling process. Chapter 4 examines the questions the client needs to address at this stage, and Chapter 5 describes several important techniques and tools which can assist the client in addressing them.

4

Enabling Clients' Understanding

At the first meeting clients will have begun to tell the counsellor their perceptions of themselves and their career situation. Whether the problem presented and explored in the first meeting is a relatively straightforward one of increasing a client's clarity about career strengths and weaknesses, or a more complex one of, for example, addressing feelings of loss and anger after redundancy, clients are usually asking, implicitly or explicitly, for clarification and self-understanding in the following areas:

● Who am I? Where am I now?
● What do I want? Where do I want to be?
● What is stopping me from moving on?

The client's own answers to these questions may be inaccurate, distorted or limited in various ways. One of the tasks of this stage is to help clients to develop a more objective and accurate self-understanding and deepen their insight into their situation. The aim is to enable clients to move towards a new and more constructive perspective which can form a basis for decision and action.

For some clients, greater self-understanding is all that is needed, and this may promote renewed energy or a change of attitude. For others, self-understanding is just the first stage. They want career counselling to help them make decisions or formulate action plans; this stage is addressed in Chapter 6.

Who am I?

At this stage the counsellor's task is to assist clients in answering the question, 'Who am I?' As outlined in Chapter 3, they will have begun to do this already through their written preparation work and initial exploration at the first meeting.

Clients may need to develop self-understanding in the following areas:

- Aptitudes (what abilities or level am I capable of attaining?)
- Skills (what can I do now?)
- Values (what is important to me?)
- Occupational interests (what am I really drawn towards?)
- Personal attributes (how does my 'personality' influence the work I do?)

In asking clients for their initial self-assessment, it is important to encourage them to be specific. Clients will often make vague statements:

> I enjoy reponsibility.
> I'm a creative person.
> I'm hopeless with numbers.
> I want to do something more worthwhile.
> I need a challenge.
> I'm good with people.
> I don't have enough variety in my job.

Concepts like 'creative' and 'worthwhile' can mean different things to different people. The meaning a word carries for the individual should be explored, and the client can be gently challenged if his or her own perception seems inaccurate.

The counsellor can formulate hunches about the way clients' aptitudes, skills, values, interests and personality are being used (or not) in their work. Clients can be helped to assess themselves systematically through the use of written assignments and also through using psychometric tests and questionnaires. Later, the counsellor can check out how any questionnaire results match up with earlier hunches.

Aptitudes
Clients often ask for help in assessing their talents, capabilities and potential. In the following case, Dennis was considering higher education:

> Dennis had experienced no success either at school or in work.
> His childhood had been strong on rejection and short on love.
> He had reacted by failing every exam, becoming violent, and
> indulging in excessive drinking, drug-taking and promiscuity.
> A trip from his native Zimbabwe to England resulted in a
> desire for a fresh start, following some pressure from his new
> English girlfriend. Dennis had little idea of his aptitudes, as he
> had virtually no experience of testing them out.

Although success in higher education is dependent on many factors other than aptitude, it was appropriate to give Dennis a relatively objective measure of his capabilities, which could be considered along with his interests, personal attributes and values. It emerged from the testing that his aptitudes were more suited to a practical, rather than academic, training. His dilemma of dealing with his girlfriend's pressure and using his real aptitudes and interests then became the focus of counselling.

Skills
Many people discount their skills unless they are linked to paid employment, usually their most recent job. Career counselling can help people to evaluate the skills they have gained from all parts of their lives, for example through hobbies and interests, voluntary work and service to the community, and in being 'only a housewife and mother'. This can help people to gain the confidence to transfer such skills to an appropriate work environment.

Self-assessment exercises, such as those described in Chapter 5, can be helpful in this process. Hopson and Scally (1991) present a useful classification of skills in four categories: skills with data (for example, classifying data), ideas (for example, expressing ideas orally), people (for example, resolving conflict) and things (for example, using machinery). Clients can assess the range of skills they have and rate their level of competence by using a skills inventory (see Nathan and Floyed, 1991). If the client gives a copy of the skills inventory form to someone else for an independent assessment, comparisons between the two sets of ratings can be revealing:

> Althea's sister rated her as more competent in the communication and negotiation skills area than she rated herself. After some discussion with her counsellor, Althea realised that she tended to take these skills for granted and undervalue them, probably because she had gained them within the context of being 'only' a housewife and mother, rather than through 'proper' work experience.

Values
Values in relation to work represent the degree to which a person regards his or her work as worthwhile. This 'worthwhileness' includes the amount of power, autonomy, creativity, learning, altruism, security, status and money which are sought in work.

In career counselling, it can sometimes assist clients to distinguish between their work and non-work values. For example, it may be very important for a person to express his or her creativity outside, but not necessarily in, work.

Values may not be stable in a person. A young man leaving school may decide to forgo the prospect of more academic work for the lure of his first car in a smart sales position. This gives him status among his peers, independence and money. Ten years later he finds himself out of a job, with no car and no qualifications. Or he cannot see himself getting any further with his present employer. Or, for whatever reason, money and status are no longer so attractive. As we outlined in Chapter 2, values can change at any time of life, but may particularly be affected by a major life event (for example, marriage, divorce, serious illness, redundancy, parenthood, religious conversion) or a more surreptitious transition, such as 'reaching 40'.

The following case demonstrates the way changes in personal values can be addressed in career counselling:

Peter was 30 years old and married with two children. With a successful career in sales and marketing, he had all the 'trappings' of success. But he felt restless. He was unhappy with the increasing necessity to play the 'political game' in order to advance his career. It emerged in the first meeting that he was disappointed with the way 'society had turned out'. His early faith in people had been shattered by the pushing and shoving he observed, received and was expected to give, just in order to 'get on'. He was angry that he was being challenged to drop his childhood values: 'People should help each other.'

Career counselling helped Peter address the real importance to him of these altruistic values. A good deal of confusion was highlighted in the discussions, and Peter eventually decided on a compromise which allowed for a more even balance between the 'altruistic' and 'power' values in his life.

Occupational interests

Interests – that is, activities which are enjoyable and rewarding – are a vital key to what motivates a person. Ability alone is of little use without adequate interest to back it up. Unless people can understand and articulate their real interests, they may find themselves pushed in the direction that others want. As the following case shows, interests can become buried in the pursuit of pleasing others:

Jenny had originally trained in teaching as it was 'what was expected of me' by family and teachers. 'I didn't want to be

a nurse or secretary, and teaching was the only option left.'
She did reasonably well at her job, but was quite content to
give it up when she married John. After bringing up two
children, Jenny approached a career counsellor with a lack of
direction. Although she had maintained an interest in art and
antiques since schooldays, she had never really considered
seriously the possibility of art or antiques as a career option.
Career counselling enabled Jenny to accept the legitimacy of
pursuing her real interests.

The career counsellor can help clients to assess their interests by
using some of the questions in Box 4.1.

Box 4.1 *Self-assessment of interests*

What subjects did you like best at school?
Which jobs/aspects of jobs have you enjoyed the most?
What evening classes have you attended with pleasure?
What hobbies, interests and activities do you enjoy in your
spare time?
Which of these activities would be the last you would give
up?
What do you like to read about?

Personal attributes
Although human beings are very adaptable and square pegs can
often force themselves into round holes, at least in the short term,
personality can facilitate a person's performance and achievement
in certain careers, but limit success in others, as the case study of
Clifford (the introverted sales representative: see pp. 31 and 32)
illustrated.

In the test feedback discussion, Clifford's view of himself was
challenged, when a personality questionnaire suggested he was
quite reserved and shy. Counselling established that he had
come to see himself as outgoing in order to believe that he
could be successful in sales. He had also felt very competitive
with a more outgoing younger brother, who had also been his
father's favourite. These discoveries gave Clifford the
confidence to let go of his desire to succeed in customer
contact jobs, and to seek work more in sales administration.

Many people have little more than a vague idea of the personal attributes needed for success in different stages of career development. The process of career counselling can often bring about greater clarity and self-understanding through relatively objective and supportive feedback. The following case illustrates how interpersonal and 'political' skills are often considered to be part and parcel of success:

> Jim was referred for career counselling by his employer. He had been with the same employer for twenty years, but things had turned somewhat sour recently; he had fallen out with his boss, and felt very bruised by his recent appraisal. He wanted an opportunity to assess himself in an independent setting.

When Jim entered employment, he had no idea that, in order to 'get on', he would have to do more than simply perform his job tasks to the best of his ability. It came as a shock that he was also judged on how well he fitted in, particularly as far as his immediate boss was concerned. Career counselling enabled Jim to decide that he was no longer committed to progressing within this organisation, and that he was better suited to a 'non-front-line' job.

Integrating self-understanding information

During this stage of the career counselling process, through discussion of home assignments and through the process of completing tests and questionnaires and receiving feedback, clients will be accumulating a wealth of information about themselves, and so will gain a more confident self-understanding. This forms a springboard for thinking about options for the future. For example, a client may be developing a self-perception, 'I am a very outgoing person', which helps to encourage the attitude: 'and so the implications are that in order to gain job satisfaction, I should now consider doing . . .' (things that conform to this more confident self-understanding).

The 'Job satisfiers' exercise in Chapter 5 can be especially helpful at this stage in helping the client to synthesise and summarise the self-assessment information they have accumulated.

What do I want?

During the first meeting it may be appropriate to elicit from clients any options they are considering for the future. However, a client will need an awareness of his or her occupational self before pursuing the answer to this question.

One way to elicit occupational ideas would be to suggest that clients look through a directory of occupational information (see Appendix C and Chapter 5). In many cases, however, it may be more fruitful to bring out into the open any fantasies clients may have about their future, or unfulfilled passions left over from childhood or adolescence. Such fantasies can deter the person from acting rationally. Box 4.2 lists some suggestions for doing this.

Box 4.2 *Suggestions for eliciting occupational fantasies*

- If you had a year off, how would you spend it?
- What are the three things you feel most passionate about (dream about, think about, read about, talk about, would do voluntarily)?
- If you could be anything/anyone you wanted, what/who would you like to be?
- Without thinking much about it, finish off the sentence 'I want to . . .'. (This can be done several times)
- What were your early dreams about what you might do or be when you grew up? (If the client says 'I don't know', or 'I didn't have any', follow up gently with: 'What might they have been?')

One or more of these suggestions can be tackled either in the counselling meeting, or as a home assignment.

It is important at this stage to strike a balance between encouraging clients to use their imagination and ignoring the constraints of the real world, and not brushing aside the outer, 'objective' realities of the client's life, and failing to demonstrate an understanding of the very real, practical limitations clients may face. Most career decisions are a compromise, as the following case study demonstrates:

Alistair was a highly paid but frustrated and unhappy solicitor specialising in company law. He had a strong interest in helping young people, and had considered retraining as a probation officer. However, with four school-age children and elderly parents to support, it was unrealistic to change direction completely. He eventually found some compromise outlets for the 'caring' side of his nature by moving to a job within the legal profession which involved training young solicitors, and by working at a local youth club one night a week.

Realism in decision making may subsequently be increased by relating enhanced self-awareness to accurate occupational information. An exercise (Satisfiers vs. Options) which can be used to help the client at this stage will be found in Chapter 6.

Some clients will need longer to reach the point where they are sufficiently in touch with their own desires and potential to answer the question 'What do I want?' constructively. There may also be times when, even with increased self-understanding and an idea of where they want to be, clients will feel 'stuck' when they try to think about getting what they want.

What is stopping me from moving on?

At this stage optimism and positive feelings about the future are often held in check by pessimism and negative emotions, with the net result that the client feels 'stuck'. In most blocked career situations, both external and internal constraints exist, as Carla's case demonstrates:

> Carla had already applied for six marketing jobs without success when she came for career counselling. She was telling herself, 'It's too competitive to get into.' The counsellor perceived that there was also a significant internal block operating: Carla was also telling herself, 'I'm not good enough.' Although counselling could not change the job situation, it helped to unravel the feelings and thoughts that were getting in the way of Carla acting with as much assertion and determination as she could to approach the job market. Counselling helped Carla to work on her feelings of not being good enough. She constantly put herself down; her counsellor pointed this out, and gradually Carla was able to interrupt her put-downs herself. She was given a homework exercise to write a list of the accomplishments in her life, including the difficulties she had survived and overcome. As the counselling progressed, she began to say to herself: 'Although it may take some time to get the job I want because entry is competitive, I'm as good as anyone else. I need to make a lot more applications using a variety of methods.'

Like Carla, many clients have a tendency to see constraints as external, and need help to recognise that there are internal blocks too, for example, low self-esteem, high levels of anxiety, guilt about the effects of a decision on significant others, anger and frustration about the existing situation, or ambivalence. Such a

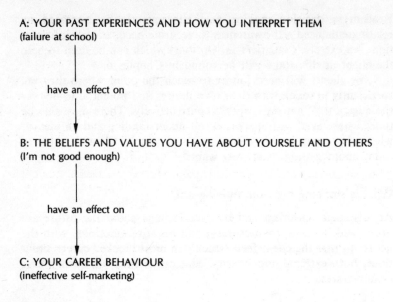

A: YOUR PAST EXPERIENCES AND HOW YOU INTERPRET THEM
(failure at school)

have an effect on

B: THE BELIEFS AND VALUES YOU HAVE ABOUT YOURSELF AND OTHERS
(I'm not good enough)

have an effect on

C: YOUR CAREER BEHAVIOUR
(ineffective self-marketing)

Figure 4.1   *Emotional triggering (Carla's example)*

recognition can enable clients to develop new and more productive perspectives for the future. In this section we examine some of the sorts of 'roadblocks' which may be in the way of clients achieving their goals, and how clients can be helped to unravel, understand and deal with various constraints.

Emotional triggering
Career counsellors need to be alert to instances where a client describes an experience which is similar in some respect to an event in the past. The recent event may act as an emotional trigger, causing the level and type of emotion associated with the early painful event to be re-experienced. For example, enabling Carla to move on involved making the connection between her current feelings, 'I'm not good enough', and past experiences of failure at school, as Figure 4.1 demonstrates.

Career counselling often needs to address 'A' and 'B' in order to change 'C'. Cathartic interventions (see Heron, 1990) are particularly appropriate in enabling the client to release painful emotion attached to past experiences when emotional triggering occurs. Some of the origins of irrational beliefs and values are now examined.

Introjected values
Introjection is a central concept in Gestalt therapy (see Clarkson,

1989). Introjected values are unquestioned (usually unconscious) values which are based on the messages clients have received from other people (often their parents) earlier in life. When people 'swallow whole' ideas of what they believe others want them to be, life becomes acting a part. The underlying message with introjected values is, 'You're only OK if . . .' (if you obey the 'shoulds'/'should nots'). Introjected values can therefore prevent people from accurately perceiving themselves and the world, which may lead to faulty career decisions.

The following case study is of a man who lost touch with his 'real self' because he learned to please his parents by becoming the sort of little boy that his parents required, in order to be loved:

> John had obtained a degree in mechanical engineering, although he found it a struggle and only achieved a third. He hated the industrial placement he had undergone as part of his studies, and did not want to pursue engineering as a career. In an emotional session, it emerged that John was given a Meccano set when he was little, and always had lots of praise and attention from his father when he did practical things. The session was cathartic, and John began to realise that he would probably survive, even if his father withdrew his love. He had a warm personality and a strong interest in helping people, and decided to investigate retraining as a massage therapist.

Some examples of introjected values which frequently occur in career counselling are listed in Box 4.3.

Many clients are not aware of their introjected values, and do not consciously state them. The career counsellor should listen very carefully for themes which indicate that an introjected value is operating, as the case studies of Paul and Stella indicate:

> Paul had started a graduate training scheme with a bank, ostensibly because his friends were all going to work in the City. However, he was never really happy from day one. After a year, he was finding it impossible to pursue alternatives, because every time he began to look at the jobs pages in the paper, he felt terrible pangs of guilt. His father had recently retired after working as an accountant for forty years.

Paul's strong introjected values were, 'Make up your mind what to do and stick to it for the rest of your working life', together with, 'Don't take risks – get a nice steady, secure nine-to-five job.'

Box 4.3 *Introjected values*

You should
- get a secure job
- be a career woman
- be perfect
- be more successful than your parents
- make upward progress within a hierarchy
- have a respectable professional job
- go to university
- get into a well-known company
- make up your mind what to do and stick to it for the rest of your working life
- get married and be a good mother
- make a lot of money

You should not
- take risks
- go into a man's/woman's job
- change direction
- be more/less successful than your parents
- waste your qualifications
- take a drop in salary

Stella was 40. With a recent divorce and two teenage children, she felt at a loss about what to do. In one career counselling session, her counsellor pointed out that she had spent more time talking about her children's career choices and her ex-husband's career difficulties than her own career future.

Stella's introjected values told her: 'Get married and be a good mother' and, 'Devote yourself to others.'

The counsellor's job is to help people see how their situation has come about, to get them to question whether their introjected values are doing them a service or a disservice, and to facilitate the release of emotion. Often it will be sufficient to reflect back the theme to the client. Counselling can also encourage the client to distinguish between their 'shoulds' and their 'wants' by gently challenging the introjected values:

John: I did all that training – it seems a waste.
Counsellor: A waste of your qualifications?
John: Yes – I should make use of them.
Counsellor: Who says?
John: My father – he keeps telling me I should stick with engineering.
Counsellor: What would happen if you did?
John: I'd become more and more unhappy.
Counsellor: It seems that your father has given you some strong messages about what you should do. Let's look at what you want to do.

For clients who have lived their whole life by 'shoulds', identifying their 'wants' may be a long-term project, and referral for personal counselling may be required.

Self-defeating beliefs

Whereas introjected values are largely unconscious and are unlikely to be directly expressed by clients, self-defeating beliefs are statements which the client will actually make (see Box 4.4).

Box 4.4 *Self-defeating beliefs*

I don't need anyone's help.
'X' will sort it all out for me.
I can't live on less than I earn now.
It's undignified to have to promote yourself.
Somewhere there's the perfect job.
There's no point planning ahead when there's so much change afoot.
Nobody will take me seriously.
Life is so unfair to me.
Everyone else is better off than me.
I won't be good enough.
It's safer not to try than to risk failure.
If I do well enough, Mum/Dad will love me.
I'll fail.
It's so competitive, I'd never get in.
Everything will be OK when I get a new job.
I can't change anything – I don't have any power.
It's too late.
If I wait long enough, things will change.
I'm too old/young/overqualified/underqualified.
I can't help the way I am – it's just the way I'm made.

Career counsellors can help clients to identify, challenge and change such beliefs, for example:

> *Client:* I won't be good enough
> *Counsellor:* What *would* be good enough?
>   Good enough *in whose eyes*?
>   Good enough *for what*?

Each challenging response by the counsellor encourages the client to look more specifically at the 'I won't be good enough' statement. 'What would be? demands a positive response. 'In whose eyes?' forces the client to identify whether there is a 'judge' left over from previous experiences. 'For what?' stimulates the client to relate the 'I won't be good enough' statement to specific criteria.

The effect of challenging interventions can be that the client is able to reassess the validity of the self-defeating belief, and develop a readiness to respond to opportunities in a more rational way.

Ambivalence

Clients often feel ambivalent about the future: it seems both exciting and frightening. Clients can be encouraged to express both positive and negative, optimistic and pessimistic sides of themselves – to acknowledge that the situation has both good and bad aspects.

Rowan (1989) has summarised evidence that there are divisions within the personality, which he calls 'subpersonalities'. Subpersonalities are recognised in common parlance by such expressions as 'being in two minds'. When two subpersonalities are in conflict, the two-chair technique used widely in Gestalt and related therapies may be helpful (see Clarkson, 1989). Clients can either be asked to write out a dialogue between subpersonalities, or the dialogue can be acted out in the counselling session. The purpose of a dialogue exercise is to help clients become more clear about attitudes and patterns which are blocking them from making a career decision. The dialogue can be between any two parts which have come up in the counselling. Some examples are shown in Box 4.5.

Box 4.5 *Dialogue exercises*

Optimist vs. Pessimist
I should vs. I want to
Ambitious vs. Lazy
I can do this because . . . vs. I can't do this because . . .
Sensible self vs. Creative self
Adventurous side vs. Cautious side
Career woman vs. Mother

This case study shows how an ambivalent client was helped by using two-chair work:

> Barry had trained and practised as a dentist in Australia. In one fell swoop, he had decided to emigrate to England, where he had a few relatives. He had left behind his parents, closest friends and his profession. He professed strong misgivings about continuing in dentistry in Britain. During the career counselling, Barry expressed a desire either to work in the travel industry or to run his own import/export business. Data from several written exercises showed him to have a strongly reserved character and a practical set of aptitudes. It emerged in counselling that he had made several poor decisions in the past, for example, in choosing the most appropriate options in his training. He had ended up feeling exhausted. Escaping appeared his only option, yet Barry also had a strong sense of guilt and feeling of obligation to continue in dentistry. The competing pressures of his guilt and fantasies led him to feel paralysed into a sense of hopelessness.

Counselling enabled Barry to address the realities of his situation by first exploring the two competing pressures through creating a dialogue between an 'I should' and 'I want' chair. This extract from a two-chair dialogue illustrates part of the process of Barry working through his ambivalence:

> *I should:* 'I really ought to stay in dentistry – think of all the time and money that was invested.'
> *I want:* 'I can't stand dealing with people. I just hate all their petty complaints.'
> *I should:* 'Look what I would be giving up – a good job with security. And people look up to me.'
> *I want:* 'Maybe patients do – but who else? I want to enjoy my work. I don't enjoy hurting people.'
> *I should:* 'But the country needs dentists.'
> *I want:* 'Not me, thanks very much!'

Whitmore (1990) describes a number of other techniques for working with subpersonalities.

A final note on dealing with blocks: no amount of 'technique' can be a substitute for good attending, listening and responding in a way which enables the client to explore and express feelings. Generally, the best way of dealing with a client's blocks is to encourage emotional expression. If blocked feelings are discharged and offloaded, the client's thinking about the future will become clearer and more positive.

Summary

In this chapter we have described the process of enabling clients to develop a comprehensive and objective understanding of the assets they have in relation to the world of work, to develop some ideas about future goals and gain insight into ways in which they may be blocking themselves from moving on. Good basic counselling skills are required throughout this process, particularly the skills of identifying themes and patterns. The career counsellor needs to be particularly alert to themes about job satisfaction (what the client finds satisfying and rewarding), and themes about blocks to action (how the person is stopping him/herself from moving on). Cathartic and challenging skills are also very important at this stage.

In Chapter 5 we examine several techniques which can be used to promote client self-understanding. These include between-sessions homework assignments, and the use of tests and questionnaires. We show how feedback can assist clients' awareness of their strengths and weaknesses in relation to the world of work. The chapter concludes with an examination of occupational information and its uses within a career counselling framework.

5

Techniques for Promoting Client Understanding

This chapter is divided into three sections. We begin by looking at the use of homework assignments between meetings. Like the preparation work clients undertake before the first meeting, exercises to encourage exploration and understanding are a powerful tool, helping people to answer the questions, 'Who am I in relation to the world of work?', 'What do I want?', and 'What's stopping me'? We will discuss the purposes of between-sessions assignments, give some examples of the types of exercise which can be given to clients, and explain how to make use of these as an integral part of the career counselling process.

In the second section we look at ways in which the timely and sensitive use of psychometric and other questionnaires (covering, for example, aptitudes, occupational interests, values and personality) can significantly assist the process of career counselling. The counsellor and client can still operate in a collaborative mode, using tests and other assessment exercises as no more than resources to stimulate discussion and to develop the client's own self-understanding. Initial contracting will have ensured, as far as possible, that clients understand this use of questionnaires.

The chapter concludes by examining the role that occupational information can play. We believe that career counsellors should not be expert providers of occupational information to clients, and we present some guidelines for making use of occupational information in ways consistent with a career counselling framework.

Using homework assignments

Any homework assignment has a number of general purposes, whilst each assignment will have its own specific purposes, relating to that particular exercise.

General purposes
First, homework maintains continuity, interest and energy, and therefore acts as a 'bridge' between meetings.

Secondly, homework gives clients an opportunity to explore a topic in more depth and in their own time.

Thirdly, undertaking homework assignments implies that career counselling is not an event but a process, taking place over a period of time. During the contracting stage, clients will have understood that career counselling is not a number of sessions which they passively 'attend' and then go away and forget about until the next meeting, but a process of thinking through and trying to make sense of past experience and present circumstances before considering the future. It involves self-analysis, decision making and action, which clients will have begun before the first meeting and which extend beyond their final meeting. The exercises and the counsellor are there to help, support and challenge clients during this period.

A fourth and related purpose is that homework puts the client in the driving seat rather than the passenger seat, as an active participant in the process. It builds on the work of the contracting phase in obtaining and maintaining the client's involvement and ownership of the process. Homework stresses that the client is the person who is responsible for doing the work; the counsellor is a consultant to the person going through the career counselling process – a neutral assistant who can stand back and help the client to see and integrate patterns.

Finally, homework may point up themes and issues which are relevant to the client's career problem, either in the content itself, or in the process. Homework exercises are a sample of work, and there is useful information to be gleaned about the client from the way in which a task is approached. The manner in which clients present their homework is often as revealing as the actual content, and can be a key to important counselling issues:

> Paul's homework exercise consisted of six sheets of immaculately typed, very detailed work, enclosed in a neat folder. His counsellor almost gave him an A+ on the spot! A significant career issue for Paul was his perfectionism arising from need for approval.

> Stella came in for her session rather breathless and dishevelled saying, 'I didn't have much time to get my homework done!' She scrabbled about in the bottom of an untidy briefcase to retrieve several dog-eared sheets covered in scrawled notes. Her chaotic approach to the exercise reflected the chaos of her life, both in and out of work.

Specific purposes
It may be appropriate to give clients an exercise for a specific

purpose, relating to the point reached in the career counselling process as well as to meet individual client needs. If, for example, low self-esteem seems a block to career choice or career development, it might be helpful to give clients an exercise of writing down ten things they like about themselves.

Examples of exercises The exercises described below are not meant to be prescriptive, but will be used to highlight certain principles, and show how homework can fit into the process of career counselling.

Self-validation

Purpose: To raise self-esteem, and develop a more positive self-image which can be related to future options. Clients with low self-esteem tend to focus on their bad points. This exercise asks clients to list their positive attributes – things they like about themselves but which are not usually in the foreground of their awareness because they tend to be taken for granted or simply never thought about.

Method: 1 Suggest categories of qualities, such as 'physical', 'mental' and 'social', or ask clients to think of situations when they feel good about themselves. Examples of qualities include strength, appearance, coordination (physical), problem solving and creative abilities (mental), friendliness and warmth (social).

2 Another way of encouraging clients to bring out the qualities they like in themselves is to ask them to complete, say, ten sentences, beginning with 'I feel good about myself when . . .'

Roland was initially stumped when asked to identify ten things he liked or valued in himself. However, with gentle but firm encouragement from his career counsellor, he realised that he appreciated his dress sense, his tennis-playing ability, his sensitivity to the plight of stray animals and his knowledge of malt whiskies! This positive discussion about himself led

Roland to value more openly some aspects of himself which he had tended to discount. He also realised that he needed to be doing work with a higher physical component.

Enjoyable events

Purpose: Many people tend to forget about their 'highs', or take them for granted. The purpose of this exercise is twofold. First, to remind clients of positive experiences that may have been forgotten; this can be uplifting, particularly if clients see their current situation as rather gloomy. Secondly it helps clients to identify any patterns of enjoyable events, such as 'the importance of working closely together with others', which may assist with career planning,

Method: The client is asked to list a number of enjoyable events and to identify what was enjoyable about them. The client is also asked to identify any qualities used, and to attempt to draw out important themes. For example, rock climbing may require physical fitness, organisation, cooperative team effort.

A depressed client may need encouragement from the counsellor to bring out these memories. It may help to suggest that a client 'thinks small' by saying, 'Your enjoyable event does not have to be a huge thing or something where you were judged by another person. It should be something *you* enjoyed.'

Sometimes patterns are very obvious to clients and they will instantly describe the main themes. For other clients the themes really need to be drawn out through discussion. Sometimes the exercise creates a surprise:

Jan had been working in a fairly solitary occupation as a researcher, and had always thought she was someone who preferred to work alone. She was surprised to find a strong theme of enjoying being with people and engaging in joint projects.

This exercise can put clients in touch with their real selves. When people are in a state of 'enjoying', they are likely to be intuitive, able to be truly themselves, and most free from the influence of their 'introjected values' (see Chapter 4). From this position, clients are more likely to be able to identify in an instinctive way important themes and directions for the future. Clearly, responsibilities and practical circumstances have to be taken into account, and realistically most people do not earn a full-time living from doing something they enjoy all the time. It is likely that clients will have to compromise to some degree:

Judy had been good at art at school, but was discouraged from pursuing it as a career by her parents and teachers and had gone into secretarial work. Her 'Enjoyable events' came up with strong artistic themes, and as she discussed them she seemed to 'come alive'. At the age of 40, although she was very bored with secretarial work, as a single parent with a mortgage, she was unable to take the risk of pursuing art as a full-time career. Following career counselling, however, she did several evening classes in painting, began to produce handmade greetings cards and gained a lot of satisfaction and enjoyment from selling them at a friend's market stall from time to time. She also did a short desktop publishing course, after which she was able to obtain slightly more interesting secretarial assignments.

Satisfying achievements

Purpose: As with the 'Enjoyable events' exercise, the purpose of this exercise is to raise self-esteem by focusing on positive memories, and to identify patterns of skills which clients may want to use in their career.

Method: The client is asked to list a number of satisfying achievements and to pinpoint what was satisfying about them. It is important to stress what the client personally finds satisfying, rather than achievements that pleased other people (unless this coincides with the client being pleased as well). The client is then asked to identify the skills and qualities used, and attempt to draw out important themes. It may help the client, in thinking about the skills used, to refer to a list of skills (see Hopson and Scally, 1991).

For some clients, achievements are not necessarily to do with work:

> Paul's achievements were all leisure related (sporting success; winning prizes for gardening) although he said he felt these successes 'didn't count'. He saw himself as a bit of a 'wimp' at work, for being afraid to take risks. The counsellor pointed out that his pot-holing exploits had required great courage. Paul realised that he had been unable to take risks at work because of fear of failing his father. In the leisure sphere this didn't matter – the pressure only applied to work achievement.

The relationship between achievement and enjoyment

There is sometimes a dynamic between satisfying achievements and enjoyable events. For example, all of the enjoyable events might describe holidays and other 'time-off' activities. This might show that a person is under stress, and holidays are enjoyable because they provide a means of escape – on its own it does not show that the person is active or interested in anything other than getting away from the pressures. This dynamic may be an important counselling issue – to explore how much importance a client places on achievement, responsibility and pressure in work and leisure.

The 'Satisfying achievements' exercise is based on the assumption that career counselling is concerned with helping people to achieve more success and satisfaction in their work, and that there may be a connection between what people have succeeded at in the past and what they will want to do in the future. It is, however, not necessarily true that what has been satisfying in the past is either enjoyable or an indicator of what clients *want* to do in the future, as this case study demonstrates:

> Janet was a sensitive and artistic child. She was brilliant at maths and her parents encouraged her to study it at degree level. In her final year, her father suggested she took up actuarial work as a career, and expressed great pleasure when Janet made a success of this too. Ten years later, Janet described her work as 'bleak' and the world she worked in as 'grey and colourless'. Janet was given the 'Enjoyable events' and 'Satisfying achievements' exercises to do. It became clear that although she found mathematical problems interesting, and gained intellectual *satisfaction* from problem solving, there was no sense of *enjoyment* for her in what she did. Her enjoyable events mostly involved people and participation in the arts. She was able to see that she had spent many years

pleasing her father, and decided it was time to please herself
– as she described it, to take a more 'colourful road'.

Job satisfiers

Purpose: For clients who are at the stage of having
accumulated information about themselves from
homework assignments and tests, this exercise
helps them to synthesise and summarise the information, then to consider the implications for their
future career.

Method: Clients are asked to consider their work
preferences and other factors which are necessary
for their job satisfaction, by reviewing the data
they have gathered about themselves from all
sources, and listing the specific elements they
want in their next job. The following case study
illustrates the outcome of such an exercise.

Jan's post as a researcher with a public service organisation
was 'deleted' at a time when she was looking around for
another job, as she was so dissatisfied at work. She wanted to
be able to understand the reasons for her frustration, as well
as establishing a career direction for the future. By the final
meeting, with some help from the career counsellor, she had
synthesised all the self-understanding information she had,
and produced the list of 'Job satisfiers' in Box 5.1.

Box 5.1   *Jan's 'Job satisfiers' exercise*

Work providing intellectual stimulation
Work making use of analytical skills
Work making use of oral/written communication skills
Work making use of organisational skills
Solving complex problems
Collaboration with colleagues
Freedom to set own schedule and work at own pace
A clear role responding to a felt need in the organisation
Work which has an impact on decision making
Work where high standards are valued
A visible, central role (not 'backroom')
An innovative, progressive environment

Clearly, such a list represents something of an ideal, almost impossible to obtain in full measure in any career. However, it is a useful list which can form a basis for evaluating the suitability of various future options for a client (see Satisfiers vs. Options exercise in Chapter 6).

Integrating the exercises into the counselling

It is important to allow sufficient time between meetings for clients to complete their assignments. In the gaps between sessions clients can also discuss their thoughts with a partner, friend or other significant person.

As well as addressing the content of the homework ('What did you learn or gain from it?'), clients can be asked how they felt about doing an exercise. For some clients, an exercise may involve confronting aspects of themselves or their past which may be difficult or painful to face. If painful feelings have been raised, this may need to be explored in the next meeting. In some cases, clients may make an attempt to do an exercise but be unable to complete it. Not all clients will wish to delve into the issues that are blocking them, and it may be possible in any case to make a 'good enough' career decision without opening up painful areas (see Chapter 7).

When a client has decided to take psychometric tests (see next section), it is helpful to begin the feedback session with some discussion of the outcome of the 'Satisfying achievements' and/or the 'Enjoyable events' exercises. Such a discussion can set the scene: the themes which emerge from the exercises can then be related to themes arising from the test feedback. For example, in the case of Jan, her strong need to work closely with others emerged as a theme from the 'Enjoyable events' exercise and was echoed later in results from personality and occupational interest questionnaires.

We hope that these few exercises give a flavour of how homework assignments can be used in career counselling. To stimulate the imagination, a larger selection of exercises will be found in Nathan and Floyed (1991).

Using tests in career counselling

The benefits of using tests in career counselling

There *are* ways in which timely and sensitive use of psychometric and other questionnaires can significantly assist the process of career counselling. Such an approach can:

- provide a framework for dialogue;
- increase clarity and confidence;
- provoke new personal insights;
- assist long-term perspectives;
- reduce the risk of haphazard decision making;
- help to explain past behaviour at work.

Provide a framework for dialogue The power of the printed word can be put to good use in career counselling. The fact that clients are asked to rate themselves on a scale of 1–10 for 'reserved – outgoing' can produce a rich discussion more easily than, to put it bluntly, the counsellor saying, 'I would like to discuss with you how reserved or outgoing you are.'

The dialogue is further enhanced if clients are asked to make their own self-assessment first. It is through this self-assessment that clients are encouraged to take responsibility, thereby avoiding casting the counsellor in the role of judge.

Increase clarity and confidence By being able to check self-perceptions on a variety of personal qualities, clients can come to be able to make quite confident statements about themselves. Discussion of test results, followed by further reflection and a subsequent counselling meeting, can lead to a confirmation of the client's self-view as well as acceptance of any surprises that emerge.

Provoke new personal insights Some test results may enable clients to see themselves or the possibilities in a new light:

Kathy (see pp. 53, 55) never fully appreciated her verbal capabilities. Aptitude tests showed a marked verbal superiority over her other aptitudes and the general population. Since she had not done well in her accountancy degree, this result and the ensuing counselling encouraged Kathy to trust this ability more. She began to consider careers where she might use her verbal abilities.

Assist long-term perspectives When a client comes to accept an aspect of him or herself, plans can be made for the future with the expectation that this characteristic will still be there in years to come. Alternatively, a clearer self-view following the use of tests can give a sense of control over the future which did not exist before.

Reduce the risk of haphazard decison making The structure provided by the systematic and comprehensive aura of tests and questionnaires can help clients to put their thoughts in order, and reduce the tendency to make decisions in a state of panic.

Help to explain past behaviour at work   'That explains it' is not an uncommon remark from clients who begin to see patterns emerging from test results and other exercises used in career counselling. For example, it may be that aptitude tests have shown that a person thinks quickly, but finds expressing thoughts in words is more difficult. Or a theme may emerge showing a preference for working with others rather than alone. This can explain why a person has been unhappy with a solitary occupation or self-employment.

How and when to introduce tests into the career counselling process

To enable tests to be seen by clients as an integral part of the career counselling process, they should be presented alongside other self-assessment and homework assignments, as resources which can provide evidence of patterns or themes of significance to the client. In the context of a collaborative counsellor–client relationship, they can be seen as just one more source of information.

Initial contracting can ensure that clients know about the fallibility of tests and that there is no question of 'pass or fail'. If clients are to be involved in a discussion of their expected results (prior to being given the actual scores), this can be mentioned as well. A written Guidelines sheet can be given out explaining what to expect at the test session (see Appendix A).

Tests should not be given to clients before the first meeting. A meeting can provide a basis for deciding whether tests are likely to be of use for this client at this time. Occasionally, a client's degree of anxiety about his or her test performance will be so strong that counselling without testing might be more appropriate. This can be judged more accurately by a face-to-face meeting than by simply reading a client's written preparation.

Types of test and questionnaire used in career counselling

Although several different types of tests and questionnaires will be described here, we do not propose a lengthy description. The British Psychological Society has produced a comprehensive review of tests which are in common use for career development purposes (see Newland Park Associates, 1991).

Aptitude tests   These tests have normative data, that is they have been tested on a random or representative population. A person's performance on the test is compared with that of others, and a 'profile' produced of relative strengths and weaknesses. Typical areas measured include abstract, verbal and numerical reasoning.

Such tests must be both (a) *valid* – a test must measure what it purports to measure; and (b) *reliable* – it should provide a reasonably consistent indication of ability over time. Every test should be accompanied by a manual, describing any research undertaken and giving figures for reliability and validity, and details of the population(s) on which it has been standardised. The technical aspects of test construction are well covered by Anastasi (1988).

A differential aptitude test can help to address the following kinds of question:

- Does the client learn better 'on the job' or through more academic means?
- Does the client have a stronger potential for working with figures or words?
- How quickly can the client think on his or her feet?
- Is the client more able to solve problems by grasping the 'whole' or by exploring the details?

Interests, values and personality questionnaires Some questionnaires available are 'normative', that is the client's 'scores' are compared with a general or particular population. For example, an individual's responses may indicate a greater liking for contact with people than the majority of the population. Other questionnaires may provide scales of particular characteristics as a way of systematically presenting the client's disparate answers to many questions. For example, one values questionnaire (Allport et al., 1960) presents 'theoretical', 'economic', 'social', 'aesthetic' and 'power' value categories.

An occupational interests questionnaire may be based on Holland's six categories (Holland, 1983). Holland defined six types of people – Realistic, Intellectual, Social, Conventional, Enterprising and Artistic, and six corresponding types of work environment. According to his theory, people seek out or create work environments which allow them to express their personalities and values. For example, people of the Enterprising orientation prefer to seek out environments which provide opportunities for persuading, dominating or leading others.

Questionnaires focusing on personality or other personal qualities may address a variety of dimensions, such as 'extroversion–introversion', 'imaginative–practical', and 'logical–intuitive'.

It can be useful to ask clients to rate themselves on the personality dimensions prior to discussion of the actual scores. The counsellor can try to draw out the themes or patterns emerging, and relate these to patterns that emerge from any homework assignments.

Dangers of using tests in career counselling

Excessive emphasis on test interpretation   It is unfortunately attractive for career counsellors to show off their 'expertise' by using words and interpretations with which they are familiar, but which have little meaning for the client. Such an excessive emphasis on interpretation is unlikely to allow the expression of the client's *feelings* about the results. Furthermore, this will discourage a client from being proactive and encourage passivity.

It is important to reiterate that any assessment tools used in career counselling are proffered as resources to aid *self*-assessment. Inevitably, some clients will *want* to read more into test results than is warranted. The counsellor should then be careful to place the results in context, and refer to the client's self-perceptions as the primary focus for discussion. Occasionally it may be necessary to make light of the tests with a comment such as, 'These question-naires are, after all, only feeding back to you what you have put into them, but in a structured format.'

Every care must be taken not to misuse the power and trust invested in the counsellor.

Tests dominating the counselling   Clients can be very gullible and naive regarding the acceptance of test results, and it can be seduc-tive to allow tests to dominate the discussions. This is especially true when there is a lack of time available, because of pressures to see a large number of clients. Insufficient training of counsellors can also lead to an excessive reliance on what, after all, are only partly accurate results. The British Psychological Society has rightly brought in a Certificate of Occupational Testing, which may go some way to reducing the misuse of those insufficiently validated and unreliable instruments now on the market which can be seen by clients as 'proper tests'.

Other client characteristics, such as lack of interest in pursuing the discussion of 'problems', in favour of a 'quick-fix solution' can pressurise counsellors to rely too much on test results. After all, clients have a right to their results, may be looking forward expec-tantly to receiving them, and might, unless sufficiently forewarned in initial contracting, secretly hope for some magical answers to emerge.

Tests are not appropriate for every person Even if a test has been properly validated (that is, the test has been shown to be measuring what it says, within certain statistical margins of error), it may not be sufficiently appropriate for a particular client. This could be because:

– the client does not fully understand the questions, perhaps because the client's first language is not English;
– the client answers the questions randomly;
– the client does not feel well on the day of testing;
– the client wants to make a particular impression.

Confusion of interests and abilities Being good at something does not guarantee an interest in the subject. It can be too easily assumed by clients that a so-called high score on an 'Interests inventory' means that a client will be 'good' at the activity or occupation. Similarly, a high score on an aptitude test does not necessarily mean an equally high level of interest.

Tape recording the feedback discussions
Because tests provide a large volume of information which clients then have to sift through and integrate into their own self-assessment, we have found that tape recording the feedback discussion has enormous benefits:

● It provides a live record of an important and unique inter-action for the client.
● It can be listened to days, weeks, months or even years after the actual meeting.
● It can be shared with a significant other person.
● It diminishes the emphasis on the 'pieces of paper' (the results).
● It enables the client to hear more of what was discussed at a time when he or she is not so closely involved.

Clients can be asked to bring their own tape to the meeting, while the career counsellor provides the recording equipment. This clarifies that the client rather than the counsellor 'owns' the tape, that is that the test results are the client's, rather than the counsellor's property.

Whilst taping has a lot to recommend it, it is important for the career counsellor to be comfortable with the idea, and for the client to be given encouragement to accept taping, but also the freedom to reject it.

Clients' thinking often moves forward considerably following a test feedback session. Many thoughts, feelings and ideas are triggered by listening to the tape. Some reactions not obviously connected with the career counselling may come up when clients listen to their tapes. Comments on voice production are quite often made; for example, 'I never realised I sounded like that' (loud, quiet, aggressive, talkative, negative). Some of these comments can provide useful data for counselling.

Once a tape has been made, it can be used to stimulate the client to prepare for the next meeting. Clients can be asked to write their reflections, thoughts, ideas and feelings on listening to the tape. They may also want to share the tape with someone close to them, or a person involved in their decision making. To encourage a continuing proactive role in the career counselling, clients can be asked to prepare an agenda for the following meeting. Such an agenda might include, for example, questions for further clarification of test information, the client's response to the tape, and considerations for action.

The benefits of taping are consistent with the values of counselling which encourage clients to take responsibility for their own decisions. As much as anything else, taping can help to further client self-understanding as a preparation for action.

Using occupational information

By this stage of the career counselling process, clients should have been disabused of any notion that the career counsellor is a matchmaker, that is, a person who will translate information about the client into the perfect 'career match', and who will know all there is to know about that occupation (and all others too). However, in order to make a decision about what course of action to pursue, the client does need information about options (for example, education and training, related career options, job opportunities, career pathways within an organisation, alternatives to traditional careers). Clients need information about what they would like to do (given their interests, personality and values) and what they can do (with their capabilities, skills and qualifications). Good information will enable the client to assess him or herself in relation to various options.

Many career counsellors feel anxious about the topic of occupational information. This is understandable: there is a bewildering amount of occupational information available, of varying quality, in various media and from a variety of sources. One reference book widely used in the United States, *The Dictionary of Occupational*

Titles (US Department of Labor, 1977), lists 22,000 different occupations/job titles. With the best will in the world, it is just not possible to keep abreast of all the information about career possibilities.

We believe that it is more realistic to consider the career counsellor as a 'general practitioner' with respect to knowledge of the world of work. Familiarity with job classification families, levels of entry and types of educational/training opportunities is important (see Boxes 5.3, 5.4 and 5.5).

Career counsellors should also have a knowledge of how to access information. Like a general practitioner, at times it will be necessary to refer clients to 'consultants', people who have detailed knowledge of particular careers. Appendix C lists a number of sources of occupational information.

The role of information
Information may be particularly appropriate when:

- clients need to consider the realism of their ideas, in terms of entry requirements (for example, am I qualified to train as a solicitor?)
- clients feel constrained within an occupation (for example, what else can a teacher do except teach?)
- clients have narrow ideas and want to broaden their horizons (for example, I've always worked with animals – what other careers are there?)
- clients' ideas are dictated by glamorous or romantic notions (for example, what is it really like to work in the travel industry?)
- clients need to develop more confidence in the suitability of an occupation before embarking on training (for example, is physiotherapy suitable for me?)

It is helpful to consider information which the client may already possess. The individual's socioeconomic backgound is one of the main determinants of this:

Julie was a languages graduate from humble origins: her father was a factory foreman and her mother a cleaner. She was the first person from her family to go to university. During her third year, she panicked about her choice of career. Occupations where she could make direct use of her languages, such as interpreting or publishing, seemed very mysterious. She eventually went into teaching, not because the

---

Box 5.2 *Suggestions for generating career options*

Recall memories of early ambitions.

Draw your ideal job situation and then look at what it represents.

Circle job ads that appeal.

List jobs of every friend/relative/neighbour you know and choose six that have some appeal.

Highlight jobs that appeal in the index of a careers directory (*Jobfile, Occupations*, etc.: see Appendix C).

Brainstorm ideas with a friend.

Ask everyone you know for ideas about what they could see you doing.

Look up articles in careers reference books for all the ideas you have had – *Occupations* lists similar careers, for example a client who is interested in architecture will find civil engineering, surveying and landscape architecture suggested.

For a week, as you watch television or see other people at work, note down jobs that appeal to you.

Consider creative alternatives too, for example self-employment; franchising; voluntary work; combining two part-time occupations (such as teaching and writing). See Nathan and Syrett (1983).

---

job had any real appeal, but because she was familiar with it, having been in a classroom herself. Interpreting and publishing felt like 'worlds apart'. She came for career counselling after she failed her first teaching practice.

A young man from an upper-class professional background who wants to enter a manual trade will be at as much of a disadvantage as this working-class graduate with no family tradition of professional work on which to draw when considering future options.

Generally, it is appropriate to encourage clients to broaden their ideas about occupational possibilities and cast a wide net initially, before narrowing down the options and assessing a 'shortlist' in detail.

Helping the client to generate options
At this stage a classification scheme can be a useful aid for clients to generate ideas. One example is CLCI – the Careers Library Classification Index – used in careers libraries and in some directories of occupational information. Another is John Holland's

categories (Holland, 1983), to which we referred earlier (see p. 83). These schemes can broaden ideas: for example in the CLCI, looking up banking will lead the client to section N, where information on other careers in finance will also be found.

To help clients think creatively, try to develop a light-hearted approach. Some methods are listed in Box 5.2.

What information does the career counsellor need?
Career counsellors should know about sources of information (see Appendix C) and have at least a general knowledge of careers, for example of job areas, levels of entry and the types of training and education which are available. Box 5.3 lists 'families' into which jobs can be classified. Box 5.4 lists a framework of job levels, devised according to the entry qualifications, amount of training and study typically required. Rather than knowing about every course in existence, career counsellors should be familiar with types of training and education opportunities; Box 5.5 provides a list.

Box 5.3 *Job areas*

- Armed Forces
- Administration, business management and office work
- Art, craft and design
- Teaching and cultural activities
- Entertainment and recreation
- Catering and other services
- Health and medical services
- Social and related services
- Law and related work
- Security and protective services
- Finance and related work
- Buying, selling and related services
- Business and management services
- Sciences
- Engineering
- Manufacturing industries
- Construction and land services
- Animals, plants and nature
- Transport

From JOBFILE '92 compiled by JIIG–CAL and published annually by Hodder and Stoughton Limited.

Box 5.4　*Job levels*

- *Mainly unskilled jobs* (for example, labourer, porter, car park attendant), needing no qualifications and only a little 'on the job' training;
- *Mainly semi-skilled jobs* (for example, driver, machine operator), not usually needing qualifications; training takes 3 months–one year;
- *Skilled jobs, manual and non-manual* (for example, building and engineering craft jobs, hairdresser, typist), often needing some qualifications. Training is 1–3 years, and some part-time study is common;
- *More skilled and specialised occupations* (for example, bank clerks, technicians, secretaries), needing qualifications with good grades. Training is 2–3 years or more, and full- or part-time study is important;
- *Semi-professional and managerial occupations* (for example, chiropodist, merchandising manager), requiring advanced qualifications, such as A levels and a 2–4 years' training period;
- *Graduate professional occupations* (for example, teacher, scientist, lawyer, engineer), needing good A-level grades, plus 3–5 years' study for a degree or equivalent qualification

From JOBFILE '92 compiled by JIIG–CAL and published annually by Hodder and Stoughton Limited.

Box 5.5　*Training and education opportunities*

- Adult residential course
- Distance learning courses
- Institutions of higher education welcoming mature students
- Occupations particularly amenable to retraining
- Areas of skill shortage
- Local employment, retraining and education opportunities
- Grants and loans available
- Details of education advisory agencies
- Details of other local advisory agencies (for example TECs for free business advice and training)

Sources of occupational information

The most valuable source of occupational information is clients' first-hand work experience (which will inevitably be limited). Reference books can only give factual information (see Box 5.6) rather than a real flavour of the work.

Box 5.6 *Categories of information found in reference books*

What the work involves
Typical working environment
Pay and conditions
Opportunities
Prospects
Personal attributes required
Qualifications required for entry
Training
Late entry
Addresses for further information (professional bodies, etc.)

Psychosocial information is occupational information which gives more of an idea of what the job is really like than the information found in books and pamphlets. The kinds of question not usually addressed in careers books include the following:

- How is the same occupation different in a small rather than a large organisation? (For example, a woman administrator who needed power and influence realised that she would be more likely to achieve this in a small organisation.)
- How will the company or career culture fit in with the individual's identity? (For example, a mechanical engineer who was gay felt very uncomfortable in a factory environment.)
- How will the requirements of a job affect both partners in a relationship? (For example, a firefighter married a woman who could not come to terms with the degree of risk involved.)
- What are the patterns of interaction with others? (For example, a secretary who was promoted to the position of office manager found that her friendships with the people who were no longer her peers were affected.)
- What is the occupational lifestyle, and will it allow the client to have the overall lifestyle he or she wants? (For example, occupations involving evening or weekend work are likely to cause difficulties for a person who plays competitive tennis.)

This information is more difficult to pin down. It is most likely to be found in other people's heads! There are complexities because occupational experiences are so variable that many different patterns of needs, personalities and lifestyle preferences can be satisfied. For example, within the occupation of counsellor, some people work as a member of a team, others in isolation, with no colleague support; some have relatively brief or superficial contact with lots of people; others have intensive, long-term relationships with a very small number of clients. Here are some methods of obtaining psychosocial information:

1. Visits, observation, work shadowing, voluntary, part-time or temporary experience

> Joseph was interested in physiotherapy and wanted to know more about whether it would suit his personality. He arranged to do some voluntary work in a hospital, and visited the physiotherapy department. He spent two days 'shadowing' a physiotherapist at work, and asked a lot of questions. After discussing the experience with his counsellor, he decided to apply for training.

2 Interviewing a person in an occupation

> Freddie had had a successful experience of teaching his wife to drive, and wondered about becoming a driving instructor. He arranged to talk to a driving instructor about the work and, with the help of his counsellor, prepared a list of questions to use as a basis for interviewing her.

Some examples of fruitful questions for clients to ask are listed in Box 5.7.

In his next session with the counsellor, Freddie said that he had been very struck by what the driving instructor had said about coping with nervous drivers and the need for patience. It appeared that his wife was a 'born driver' and had made rapid progress, passing her test at the first attempt. He felt that he would not enjoy dealing with people who were 'failures', and decided to abandon the idea.

3 Professional bodies/trade associations – for example, the Law Society for information about legal careers.

4 Personal contacts: parents, partners, relatives, colleagues, ex-colleagues and friends (together with *their* contacts) may be valuable sources of occupational information.

Box 5.7 *Information interviewing*

Examples of questions

Why did you choose this as a career?
What is a typical day like?
How many people do you meet in an average week? What types of people?
What do you like best about the job? What is most rewarding?
What do you like least about the job? What is most stressful?
If you could change the job to give you more job satisfaction, what changes would you make?
What sort of person is best suited to this job?
How does the job affect your life outside work?

Generally, the further away information gets 'from the horse's mouth', the less valuable it becomes.

Occupational information: guidelines for the career counsellor

1 Ensure that clients understand that they are responsible for doing their own research.
2 Avoid using the career counselling session as a vehicle for feeding information to a client. There is a danger of confusing the contract.
3 Help clients to understand job classification families and levels of entry (Boxes 5.3 and 5.4) and show them how to generate a list of career possibilities.
4 Direct clients to relevant formal and written sources of information which are likely to be dispassionate and objective, and also to informal, oral sources where possible.
5 Encourage and support clients in the process of researching career options in detail.
6 Help clients to relate the occupational information as objectively as possible to their self-assessments. For example, a client who is very attracted to being a solicitor but not very articulate may try to persuade himself that he is articulate when he reads that this is one of the qualities required.
7 Help clients to evaluate the information, and caution them about the inaccuracy or incompleteness of some information. For example, most occupational information is geared to school

leavers, and entry requirements may be different in practice for mature entrants.

8 Support clients in dealing with their emotional reactions when gathering information.

Researching occupational information may produce surprising insights for a client, and lead to a revision of the self-concept:

> Carolyn had been working as a sales representative and was considering training as a social worker, until she did some investigation into the level of student grant and of starting salaries when qualified. She had not expected the work to be well paid, but was very shocked when she realised the sacrifices which would be involved if she was to pursue this career. She also needed support to talk through her discovery of how important economic values actually were to her when it came to the crunch.

Labour market information

Information about employment trends and forecasts of shortage occupations dates very rapidly and is not widely available in reference books. Occasional reports are produced, for example, by the Department of Employment (see Skills and Enterprise Network, 1991), but it is best obtained from more ephemeral sources, such as newspaper articles, or from interviewing experts rather than from books. It can also be misleading. Trends do not last; people who decide to train in a shortage occupation now may find that by the time they are qualified, there is a glut.

In addition, generalisations about declining sectors do not necessarily mean that a particular client will not be successful in applying for a position in such a sector. Clearly, success is more likely if the client is well motivated, competent, has good job-hunting skills and is prepared to relocate.

Summary

This chapter has considered techniques to promote clients' understanding of themselves. Methods described have been self-assessment exercises (completed by clients as 'homework' between meetings), undertaking psychometric tests and other questionnaires, and researching the requirements of occupations so that clients can relate their self-understanding to occupational possibilities. We have stressed the importance of ensuring that such techniques, and particularly the interpretation of test results, are used in a way which is consistent with the values of counselling, where clients are responsible for decision making.

The final phase of the career counselling process, enabling clients to use their enhanced self-understanding to make decisions and formulate action plans, is addressed in Chapter 6. Endings, support and follow-up will also be discussed.

6
Action and Endings

This chapter extends the discussion of techniques of promoting self-understanding to the final phase, the point when clients are ready to end the career counselling relationship, either temporarily or permanently. This may mean that clients want some plan of action to take away. Different understandings of 'action' and the construction of action plans will be discussed.

The closer clients come to a decision, the more they may experience and show 'resistance'. The feelings associated with such resistance and ways of enabling clients to manage this stage will be discussed, together with exercises to assist clients in moving towards a decision.

The career counselling process does not necessarily end at the final meeting, although the progress clients have made towards meeting their objectives for the career counselling can and should be reviewed at this stage. Ways of encouraging clients to maintain momentum and put their plans into action will also be discussed.

Decision-making and action

Counsellor and client have reached the final phase of the career counselling process. Good contracting earlier on will be of great value now. It is likely, however, that whatever was contracted earlier, the client will come expecting to 'move on' in some way and to end the meeting with something tangible to take away.

What is action?
The word 'action' is somewhat limiting in describing this stage. The expectation could easily be that the choice is either between, resignedly, staying put in the current career, or making a complete change of career. Box 6.1, however, indicates the variety of actions that can take place.

Some of these changes may affect each other, for example, increasing the emphasis placed on life outside work may decrease the discomfort felt in work. Clients may not be fully aware of the possibilities available to them, and showing them Box 6.1

Box 6.1   *Varieties of actions*

- Change in attitude and approach to current job.
- Increase self-expression outside work (for example, take up writing/art).
- Seek development within organisation (for example, secondment, project work, job rotation, becoming a mentor).
- Change department, but to a similar job.
- Change job within the organisation (for example, from laboratory work to sales).
- Change organisation, but stay in same career.
- Change from full-time to part-time or freelance employment (possibly developing a new career in spare time).
- Start own business in spare time (perhaps extending a hobby).
- Take new job as a 'stepping stone' to new career – for example (a) within the organisation: sales to marketing; (b) outside the organisation: from banking to public relations via financial public relations.
- Change career by retraining (for example, Open University MBA).
- Change career by promoting transferable skills (for example, teacher to trainer).

---

might succeed in prompting greater awareness and a more creative approach to thinking about the future.

Many clients will want at least to consider alternative career scenarios, even if they end up rejecting them. The counsellor can enable clients to do this by giving written assignments which can aid the consideration of options and enable a decision to be made.

Choosing between options: written exercises
The first exercise – 'Satisfiers vs. options' – is appropriate to give at the time when the counsellor senses that clients are in a position to make a sufficiently rational assessment of what they want in a job. If this is not the case, the guided fantasy exercise described later in this chapter is more suitable. Guided fantasy may also suit clients who respond to a more intuitive approach. The other exercises in this section may be useful in coming to a decision about a possible option which has been identified through the first exercise.

Box 6.2   *'Satisfiers vs. options': Jan's ratings*

Job satisfiers

Options	1	2	3	4	5	6	7	8	9	10	11	12	Total
Last job	7	10	7	9	8	4	9	1	6	4	2	2	69
Same occupation, different organisation	9	9	9	10	9	10	5	10	9	8	9	7	104
Previous job (for comparison)	5	2	9	10	3	8	2	10	3	8	7	6	73
Market research	5	6	6	6	5	5	4	6	8	7	8	7	73
Employment research	7	10	7	7	6	6	9	7	5	7	6	7	84
Academic research	7	10	6	7	7	6	9	6	4	8	5	6	81
Info. manager (NHS)	7	9	10	10	9	9	6	10	8	7	9	9	103
Info. manager (education)	7	9	10	10	9	10	6	10	8	7	9	7	102
Systems analyst	7	9	8	9	10	7	6	10	8	8	7	7	96
Self-employment (consultancy)	8	9	10	9	7	4	10	9	6	10	8	8	98

Key to job satisfiers in Box 6.2

1 Intellectual stimulation
2 Using analytical skills
3 Using oral/written communication skills
4 Using organisational skills
5 Solving complex problems
6 Collaborating with colleagues
7 Freedom to set own schedule
8 Responding to a felt need
9 Impact on decision making
10 Organisation values high standards
11 Visible, central (not backroom) role
12 Innovative, progressive environment

These exercises have several benefits:

- Clients may reflect and move forward on their own, independently of the career counsellor.

- Clients may produce their own ideas for discussion, thereby reducing the chances of becoming embroiled in a 'Why don't you . . ., yes, but . . .' discussion.
- The degree of thought and research put in by clients provides the counsellor with some clues to progress and the approach required in the final meeting (for example, is further counselling required? Is the client wanting to discuss practicalities?)

'Satisfiers vs. options'   The purpose of this exercise is to provide clients with a framework for considering possible options for the future, and to start assessing the degree of satisfaction they might provide. The exercise asks for the list of elements of job satisfaction produced in the 'Job satisfiers' exercise (see p. 79) to be evaluated against a number of scenarios.

Clients are asked, for each possible option they are considering, to rate on a 1–10 scale the extent to which they believe each option would offer them job satisfaction (1 = not at all; 10 = completely). It can also be useful (if possible) for the client to include their current job, a previous job they have enjoyed and a previous job they have disliked, for comparison purposes. Box 6.2 shows Jan's completed matrix (see p. 79 for her case study).

At this stage generating energy and being creative is more important than being precise. During the rating process, clients can be encouraged to give their subjective evaluations freely – even if they do not have completely accurate information about an option, they can make an estimate. Scenarios which the client rates are likely to include different careers, but need not be restricted to alternative career choices. They may include any of the suggestions in Box 6.3.

Box 6.3   *Possible scenarios for 'Satisfiers vs. options' exercise*

- Alternative career, while in training
- Alternative career, one year after training
- Alternative career, five years after training
- A combination of two activities (for example, development of creative writing while continuing in current career)
- Two part-time jobs
- Self-employment (after six months, two years, five years)
- A 'stepping stone' job
- Current job with a different boss
- Current occupation with a different employer

Other possible options may arise during counselling.

Pros and cons   When at least one reasonably attractive option has been identified, a simple pros and cons exercise (Box 6.4) can assist clients to consider the practical long- and short-term advantages of that option. The questions implicit in this exercise are:

● Of what benefit would this option be to me?
● What would I have to give up to have this option?
● How likely is it that I could get this option, given my constraints and assets?

Box 6.4   *Angela's 'Pros and cons' exercise sheet*

OPTION: Law (Training to be a solicitor)

	Pros	Cons
Short term	In London	Low income
	Be with husband	Difficult to find traineeship
	The training	Low pay
Long term	Professional qualification	Might not find type of work I want
	Be a partner	Need to take work home
	Potential earnings	Too office bound

Balance sheet   This exercise enables clients to focus on the effects of making a particular choice on the important people and aspects of their lives. Both negative and positive effects are examined, as demonstrated in Box 6.5.

In all of these exercises, it is possible to add some refinement to the preferences and consequences by weighting each of them, for example, on a scale of 1–5 in terms of their importance.

'Optimist vs. pessimist'   This exercise asks clients to have a dialogue between the optimistic and pessimistic parts of themselves. When a client seems to be 'in two minds' about a course of action, saying something like, 'I know this is right for me, but I can't seem to bring myself to do it', the 'Optimist vs. pessimist' exercise may be useful in helping clients to uncover any attitudes which may be blocking them from making a decision and

Box 6.5 *Freddie's 'Balance sheet' exercise*

OPTION: Start small business in spare time

Effects on	Negative	Positive
Wife	She may resent losing some of our quality time	She has said I need something to lift me
Children	Less time to play	They could earn some pocket money
Employer	I won't be available as before on Fridays	I may be able to supply the company
Health	May get overtired	Will get less depressed
Finances	Less money in short term	Possibly more in long term

to address any anxieties which may be preventing them from taking constructive action. See Box 6.6 for an example.

Box 6.6 *Kathy's 'Optimist vs. pessimist' exercise*

Course of Action: Start a correspondence course in journalism

Optimist: I can do this because: I have an aptitude for writing.
Pessimist: I can't do this because: I'm afraid of my writing being criticised.
Optimist: I can do this because: I have a lot of support and encouragement at home.
Pessimist: I can't do this because: I'm too busy at work.
Optimist: I can do this because: I know about time management and prioritising, and learning journalism is very important to me.

The exercise can be carried out either in writing or face to face. If conducting the exercise face to face, ask the client to acknowledge that two sides exist – the part that expects things to work out fine, and the part that expects the worst to happen. Counsellors who are confident about conducting two-chair work (see pp. 70–1 for a discussion of this useful exercise), can put the optimist and pessimist on different chairs, with a third chair being used to bring the two parts together.

Counsellors who are not comfortable with two-chair work might consider using the written approach, followed by discussion about the themes which seem to be holding the client back.

Reviewing progress

Towards the end of career counselling, a progress review enables both the client and counsellor to look back at what has been achieved. A review may serve the following purposes:

- It paves the way for ending the relationship, and prepares clients to continue their journey without the counsellor.
- It enables the client to see the career counselling in perspective.
- It strengthens the client's resolve and confidence, by highlighting the progress made.
- It underlines clients' continuing responsibility for their own development.

Although the primary objective of a review is not the evaluation of the counsellor's work, the review process may also give useful feedback to the counsellor about their work. (The evaluation of career counselling is discussed in Chapter 8.)

We have found that the feedback from progress reviews fits Oakeshott's (1991) model, which was developed in an educational guidance context, that the helping process enables clients to increase their knowledge and self-awareness and acquire a number of personal skills. These include decision-making and action-planning skills, self-confidence, and goal-setting techniques. This confirms our view that the career counselling process is educative.

It is helpful to ask clients to recall the objectives with which they began career counselling, although these may change as clients progress through the stages. Generally, many clients begin career counselling by articulating externally observable objectives, for example, having information about options. The process of review can reveal that, although clients do make some progress towards achieving such objectives, change at a more subtle level has occurred. Allen (1975) describes these as changes in:

- *internal cognitive functioning*, for example, an increased understanding of behaviour and the reasons for it, and fewer self-defeating beliefs;
- *internal affective functioning*, for example, coping more effectively with negative feelings, such as anger and bitterness about redundancy, or developing greater self-confidence.

One client expressed surprise at her boost in self-confidence:

> Career counselling channelled me into thinking about what I really enjoyed and was good at. The whole experience of guided self-examination has, to my surprise, given me a lot more confidence about actually going for what I want.

These more subtle, or internal, changes may take time to work through to (external) action, and may not be immediately visible to others. Pressure can be created for clients by well-meaning friends and relatives, who may look for tangible signs of the success of career counselling. For example, 'Well, what was the result then? – what are you going to *do*?'

Goals and action
There is often a confusion between the terms 'goal' and 'action plan'. Goals are specific statements of *what* clients aim to achieve. Action planning is *how* clients will set about achieving their goals. The temptation to rush on to the 'how' without sufficiently considering the 'what' should be resisted.

Establishing useful goals is not an easy process. An effective goal will conform to a number of criteria, summarised by the mnemonic SMART:

Specific
Measurable
Attractive
Realistic
Time-Bound

Specific   Goals are virtually useless if stated in general terms. They are likely to be as effective as a New Year Resolution like 'I must give up smoking'. On the other hand, it helps to start somewhere. The counsellor can help clients to increase the specificity of a 'statement of intent' by asking the single question 'How?' Box 6.7 gives an example of the three steps towards converting a vague statement of intent into a more specific aim and then into a very specific goal.

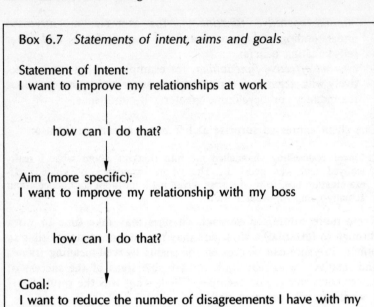

Box 6.7   *Statements of intent, aims and goals*

Statement of Intent:
I want to improve my relationships at work

how can I do that?

Aim (more specific):
I want to improve my relationship with my boss

how can I do that?

Goal:
I want to reduce the number of disagreements I have with my boss

Measurable   In addition to being specific, the goal should be measurable or verifiable. In other words, 'I will know I have achieved it when [for example] I have reduced the number of disagreements I have with my boss.'

Attractive   An attractive goal is one to which clients are committed. If the goal is for someone else, or there is another more important goal behind the one expressed, this goal will be sabotaged. An example is when clients express a desire to earn more money, whereas the hidden goal is to gain more recognition. A goal aimed at increasing salary alone may not bring the required recognition.

Realistic   Goals should not be rooted in fantasy, thus being too difficult to achieve. Nor should they be so easy to attain that clients are hardly motivated to act. Goals *should* be within the client's value system, and of sufficient significance to provide a reward on their completion.

Time-bound   Setting some time limit for achievement of goals provides a focus. Such time boundaries can act as motivators in themselves. They can also act as review dates.

The action plan

Once a good enough goal has been agreed, the client can be encouraged to think about the steps he or she needs to take to achieve it. A written action plan can be a useful way of clarifying clients' stated commitments to action, and a suggested pro-forma which can be useful to clients is given in Appendix B. There is always the danger, however, that clients will prematurely decide on an action plan without sufficient thought, either to please the counsellor or to convince themselves or a significant other person, such as a partner or a parent, that a decision has been reached.

The very act of completing such a plan on paper, after what might have been a committed and exhausting counselling experience, can act as both a reward and a spur to action. But there is a greater likelihood that action plans will be successful if the counsellor ensures that the criteria shown in Box 6.8 are first met.

Box 6.8 *Criteria to fulfil before completing action plans*

- Identify well-thought-out goals.
- Allow action plan to be owned by client.
- Indicate to client that action plan is not rigid, should be reviewed regularly, and probably revised.
- Give sufficient time to address fears of change.
- Address ways of coping with disappointment.

Addressing fears of change

All changes, even the most longed for, have their melancholy, for what we leave behind us is a part of ourselves; we must die to one life before we can accept another. (Anatole France, *The Crime of Sylvestre Bonnard*)

It should come as no surprise that clients show anxiety when approaching what they consider the 'crunch point' – a decision just has to be made. Of course, some of the techniques and exercises already described can help to reduce such anxiety or at least make it more tolerable. There are a number of contributory factors to the 'cold feet' many clients have at this point.

Clients may worry that their choice may not meet with the approval of significant others. Possibly because of past experiences of rejection, they may fear competition in the job market. There may be fears that the plan will not work (for example, a shy client who finds it hard to ask for information). Apparent 'cold feet' about making a career decision may be due to the client's decision, on reflection, that other life issues take priority (for example, adjusting to a divorce).

Further counselling may be necessary before clients are ready to implement action plans. One way of helping clients feel more at ease with a new idea is to allow them to become accustomed to the 'feel' or 'sense' of it. Doing a guided fantasy exercise can be helpful.

Guided fantasy This face-to-face exercise asks the client to live the new idea in their imagination. Box 6.9 has a suggested text for such a fantasy. The exercise requires confidence and familiarity with the use of guided fantasy techniques (see Whitmore, 1990)

Box 6.9 *Text for guided fantasy*

Begin with a short relaxation exercise. The following instructions should be read out slowly with gaps of 15–30 seconds between each sentence.

Now you feel relaxed, I would like you to picture yourself in five years' time. You feel very content with your life. You are working in –, your chosen occupation. I'd like you to imagine a typical day. You get up, really looking forward to your day. You get dressed – what are you wearing? You have breakfast and go to work – how do you get there? Are you alone or is there someone with you? You arrive at work – take a look around you before you start work. What does it look like? Are there any other people present? What are you particularly looking forward to about your day? You start your work – how do you spend your morning? [And so on.]

When they have reached the end of the day, clients can be asked to write down their fantasy.

Such an exercise can produce new ideas, rather than just flesh out an existing one. It can also give rise to strong feelings.

When she came to her final meeting, Geraldine's muddled feelings were still evident. It seemed there was some major block to moving forward, but neither she nor the counsellor knew what that was.

A guided fantasy produced two major results. First, a brand new work idea evolved, which drew on some of the (previously muddled) earlier ideas. It seemed a practical one. In addition, the discussion after the fantasy revealed the crucial block to moving forward – the confusion Geraldine felt about her desires for a child and her ambitions for career success. This discussion released Geraldine's energy, which enabled her to formulate an action plan covering both work and non-work objectives. A further meeting was arranged to review the plan after three months.

Positive self-talk Through the counselling, clients may feel encouraged to think more positively about possibilities. But negative self-talk may still prevail (see pp. 69–70). Some examples of the negative thinking which tends to occur when considering action are as follows:

● I'll never be able to do it.
● I always fail at anything new.
● I mustn't make a fool of myself.
● I'm too stupid.
● It won't work.
● Others will disapprove.

– and I'll feel angry, resentful or full of self-pity (and I couldn't bear that, I'd go to pieces).

The career counselling process itself may have the effect of reinforcing a client's decision, and thus counter some of these self-defeating beliefs. It may also be useful to encourage clients to talk to themselves more positively by asking:

'What's the worst thing that could happen?'

Or to get them to say:

'I may feel stupid, but it's not the end of the world.'

or

'I can only try my best.'

or

'The choice may not be perfect, but that's OK.'

It is helpful to ask clients to write down their negative thoughts, and then convert each thought into a more assertive and determined form of words. Box 6.10 gives some examples.

Box 6.10 *Encouraging positive self-talk*	
It's difficult for me to . . .	It's a challenge to . . .
I'll try to . . .	I'm going to . . .
I can't . . . because	I could. . . if . . .
I wish that . . .	I know that . . .
I should . . . but . . .	I will . . .
I don't want . . .	I do want . . .

Positive self-talk can help clients to reduce their feelings of compulsion about success and failure, and increase their ability to cope with disappointments after the counselling has ended. Yost and Corbishley (1987) discuss additional techniques for helping clients who are experiencing difficulties in making career decisions.

Endings

The end of the relationship between client and counsellor in career counselling may be less of an issue than the end of the counselling relationship in some types of personal counselling, for the following reasons:

1 Career counselling is usually a short-term process. The client comes for career counselling because of a particular career issue which may require a decision or action within a relatively short period.
2 The contract establishes that the meetings are a structured support to the client's own thinking and working through of the career issues brought.
3 Dependency is never encouraged within the counsellor–client relationship.
4 A series of meetings is arranged, so the end is in sight from the beginning.
5 The end of the final meeting is not the end of the career development process. The client may have an action plan, with tasks for a week, a month, three months and more.

It could be argued that, if a client were to feel bereft at the end of career counselling, the career counsellor would not have done a very good job of enabling and facilitating the client. Like the mountain guide who takes the travellers to the pass, and then leaves them to ascend to the summit alone but well equipped to undertake the remainder of the journey, at the end of the final meeting the career counsellor says 'goodbye', leaving clients equipped with the skills and confidence to pursue their action plans independently.

Anne wanted career counselling to help her assess her capabilities. She 'fell into' teaching but had never felt happy in it. She also wanted to clarify why she had found it so difficult to thrive in teaching, and find an appropriate alternative career.

By the final meeting, Anne had identified some clear work preferences – 'I like working at my own pace, with a varied work schedule. I like to work on my own, but with access to people at regular intervals. I enjoy putting things in order, interpreting numbers, working systematically and getting an end-product.' In her final meeting, Anne discussed how these preferences related to different kinds of career and work environment, and talked over her feeling of panic about the possibility of a change.

She decided in the final meeting to hand in her notice and to research alternative occupations. Becoming an accountancy technician particularly appealed to her eye for detail and order. She left the career counselling room with a sense of release from the past, and new energy for the future.

However, not all endings are so neat and tidy! Some clients will still experience feelings of loss about saying goodbye, particularly if they have had some difficult endings in their lives. It may be appropriate, at times, to provide a few extra meetings to support a client through a hard time.

Laura's husband had recently died of a heart attack. They had been married for ten years. Her mother had died of cancer two years previously. Although she had had some bereavement counselling which had been a great help, her social life had revolved around her husband and his work. The rapport between Laura and the career counsellor was strong. The career counsellor avoided a potential trap by acknowledging Laura's need for a friend, and by helping her to reconstruct a social life and develop friendships. On the career front, she decided to study for A levels and apply to university. Although she had met her career counselling objectives after four meetings, she was not ready to say 'goodbye' to yet another person, and she decided to arrange three more meetings with the career counsellor, spread over the next year.

Final meetings, too, are not always the place to tie up every loose end. Counselling skills will always be appropriate, and some final meetings may be completely taken up with working on emotional issues:

Barry's emotions (see p. 71) required a lot of attention in his final meeting. He was not ready to move on and make a decision. With a trip abroad planned, and no fixed home in this country, he was not able to leave behind his career as a dentist. Counselling had, however, enabled him to face some important issues in relation to his life and career, and had increased his resolve to sort out his life in general before making a career decision. It would have been a pointless exercise at this stage to get him to complete an action plan.

The counsellor asked Barry to write with a report on his feelings and thoughts following the counselling. In his letter, Barry was able to acknowledge that he was 'lacking any interest to follow dentistry'. There was also a glimmer of energy emerging towards a new direction: 'I've taken some limited action about starting my own business – I've written to – and spoken to –.' He admitted his fears and needs: 'I'm very scared to get financially involved and perhaps lose everything. I need more security, especially at the moment.' He was able to analyse his 'stuckness': 'I just don't seem to be able to think about such a thing – I guess that's why I'm firmly stuck in the dentistry rut and "afraid" to get out of it.'

The final meeting had focused on Barry's blocks, and the possibility of psychotherapy was discussed. The career counsellor had recommended appropriate reading, and Barry confirmed in the letter his desire to pursue some kind of self-awareness activity. 'I am prepared to give it a try on my own, but feel I may need some help in getting going.'

The ending was not clear-cut. Career counselling brought to the surface some potent issues and feelings for Barry. Not only should career counsellors be aware of and skilled in dealing with this possibility (see Chapter 7 for further discussion), they should also be aware that a client may blame the counsellor for any newly surfaced negative feelings, as Barry's letter shows:

'I feel very confused . . . almost angry and rather disillusioned with career counselling.'

But he was able to accept some responsibility in this process:

'I don't feel I have been given a very clear direction, but that's probably my fault, not yours.'

Of course, the self-defeating patterns evident in this letter match the still unresolved patterns emerging in the counselling, that is, the 'blame vs. self-blame' and 'should' vs. 'want'. But Barry still wished to continue the career counselling process with the counsellor:

'I would like to meet you again . . . and discuss things further – hopefully, by then, I'll be feeling a lot more positive about myself and my career direction.'

Continued support

People vary greatly in their need for support, but access to someone with whom they can talk over their plans and their progress is important for most clients. People need to be able to discuss the results (good or bad) of the action they have taken. Most find it helpful to have someone on their side, who believes in them and respects them, even if they are rejected. It is also encouraging to have someone to recognise and praise the little successes and achievements, and in due course to help in celebrating the completion of the action plan.

Although at this stage the primary function of the career counsellor is to enable clients to assess their support needs and decide how to go about meeting them, most clients appreciate the offer from the counsellor of further help and support in the future, should this be necessary. The majority of clients will probably not need to take up the offer, but the career counsellor should be clear about what any offer of support encompasses. It is helpful to consider the questions in Box 6.11.

Follow-up

By the end of the final meeting with the career counsellor, clients often feel in a position to move forward. Some will have made quite dramatic progress; they may see their goal in sharp focus, and feel optimistic and energised. The tasks in the action plan will

---

Box 6.11   *Offering support*

Are you offering further meetings to the client? For what purpose? How many? How often?

Are you offering telephone contact to the client? For what purpose? How long? How often?

Are you offering contact by letter to the client? For what purpose? On what basis?

Are you offering other services to the client, for example help with CV preparation, interview practice, writing a reference? On what basis?

If fees are involved, be clear about what fee is payable and what is not.

---

probably be at the forefront of the client's mind. Clients will often remark at this point 'It's all down to me now. I know what I have to do, and only I can do it'.

However, there is a danger that, on leaving the career counselling room, clients may slump back into old patterns, which often involve procrastination and delaying tactics. With the best will in the world, good intentions may fade, and competing demands may act to ensure that the action plan gradually goes further and further down the client's mental 'in-tray'. This problem of inertia should be anticipated. A number of techniques may be used to try to facilitate the career development process after the initial contract between client and career counsellor has been concluded, and to encourage and support clients in putting their action plan into practice. The techniques are all variations on the theme that while it is easy to ignore one's own good intentions, it is more difficult to ignore external reminders – people or things that the client cannot put to one side so easily.

Use of a summary   Shortly after the final meeting, the career counsellor can send a summary to the client. This can be a three- or four-page document which sums up the client's progress during the career counselling and what he or she needs to do next. It may contain the key points arising from the exercises, tests and meetings, together with the action plan. Such a summary acts as an external record of the career counselling process, and for some clients it provides a psychological link with it, Receiving the summary can sometimes fuel the process of taking action. (Incidentally, writing the summary is a useful rounding-off and letting-go process for the career counsellor – see Chapter 8.)

Other physical reminders Just pinning the action plan up somewhere visible can be a helpful reminder. Clients often spontaneously think of their own devices for prodding themselves into action. Getting organised by setting up a special work space (even if it is just a 'Career Development box file') can be useful. Some clients start a 'Career Development diary' or use a wall-planner to record their progress. Others timetable a 'career review' meeting in their diary. Clients can be asked to write a letter to themselves outlining their goals and plans and send it to the counsellor. The counsellor then posts it back to the client after an agreed interval (for example, in three months' time) to act as a reminder.

Support from others Clients can be asked to think of one or two people on whom they can rely for whole-hearted support in putting their action plan into practice. Likely people might include a partner, friend, colleague, sister or brother. Clients are encouraged to discuss their action plan with their supporter, and to arrange regular support meetings.

Follow-up meeting A further meeting with the career counsellor can be arranged in, say, three months' time to consider the progress made with the action plan, and to provide support to tackle any obstacles which have been encountered. This sort of arrangement can be helpful for clients who need to do a substantial amount of research into options before taking any decisions. It is also helpful for clients who need to address a related issue, for example divorce or bereavement, through personal counselling before they can progress with their career development. Where the time scale can be reasonably well anticipated, it is sensible to arrange a follow-up meeting at the final career counselling session.

Rewards As many counselling textbooks recommend (for example, Egan 1990), it is helpful if clients can be encouraged to build in rewards for taking various steps to fulfil their action plan. For example, after completing an application form, a client might reap the reward of reading a chapter of an enjoyable novel.

Summary

This chapter has described several techniques for assisting clients with decision making, defining career goals and planning action. Although this can be a straightforward process, clients' anxieties may be raised as they approach a decision point, so the need for the career counsellor to respond to clients' emotions right until the end has been emphasised. Different ways in which the career counselling may end have been illustrated, and various means of encouraging clients to maintain momentum after the relationship has finished have also been discussed.

The next chapter addresses a number of issues and questions the career counsellor will typically face in practice, and outlines some of the specialist knowledge required.

7

Issues and Skills for Career Counsellors

Many issues that arise in the practice of career counselling have already been raised in previous chapters. Here we will take a closer look at some of these key questions and dilemmas. Issues that commonly arise for career counsellors include the pressure to give advice, dealing with client resistance, working with 'significant others', the boundaries between career and personal counselling, referral, and how to work effectively with clients from 'minority' groups in a way that respects differences but does not reinforce stereotypes. Later in this Chapter we will sum up the particular kinds of skills and knowledge required for career counselling.

Key issues for career counsellors

Does the client need career or personal counselling?
Clients sometimes spend much of their first meeting discussing a personal issue. Apparently, if friends, colleagues and family enquire about a client's visit to a *career* counsellor, it is more socially acceptable than seeing a *personal* counsellor.

In addition, some clients come for *career* counselling consciously expecting to discuss their career, but actually use the time, sometimes to their own surprise, to discuss personal problems. If, however, the career counsellor allows the client to pursue the personal route, it is possible at the end of the meeting that a client will say or think, 'I didn't get what I came for.'

At some point, therefore, it may be appropriate to remind a client of the *career* nature of the contract. If the personal issues prove persistently dominant, it could be helpful to renegotiate the contract or discuss the possibility of a referral elsewhere (see also Chapter 3). Box 7.1 suggests some questions which may enable the practitioner to decide whether career or personal counselling is more appropriate.

The emotion a client feels about an event like redundancy is often so debilitating that it must be looked at first, as in the following case:

Box 7.1 *Some questions to clarify whether career counselling is appropriate*

- Is the emotion that a client feels about a problem so debilitating that it must be looked at first?
- Does this client have sufficient 'attention' to deal with the career issue/choice?
- Is the career issue the least of the client's problems?
- Is the client being unreasonably demanding of the career counselling process?

Timothy (see p. 29) had recently been made redundant, after twenty-five years with the same employer. He had no friends and few hobbies outside his work, and had devoted himself to work achievements, often staying well past the required time. He was not only devastated by the news of his redundancy, but was also virtually incapacitated by the anxiety he subsequently felt. In the first meeting with his counsellor, it emerged that Timothy had 'used' his work to avoid facing some earlier painful experiences.

Timothy's painful childhood needed to be addressed before he could make a rational consideration of his future, and prepare himself for anything like an effective job-hunting effort.

The reality of being out of work introduces another dilemma. The client's need to meet basic expenditures, let alone earn a decent living, does not go away! Counselling can take a length of time inconsistent with the client's sense of urgency to get a job. One expedient solution might be to give some time to the personal problem whilst the client is taking advantage of all available state benefits and becomes aware of, and possibly participates in, government-sponsored training or retraining programmes. This may reduce the client's sense of urgency whilst giving time to work on the underlying problem.

The most appropriate way forward will depend on many factors, such as the intensity of the client's reaction to the redundancy, the expectation of re-employment, and the client's own emotional and financial supports.

Sometimes the career issue seems to be the least of a client's problems, as in Joanna's case:

Joanna was 46 and had a reasonably successful career as a

features journalist. She had even been able to combine this work with her interest in health and complementary medicine. However, since her husband had left her two years earlier, she had experienced periods of deep depression, along with a strong desire to 'find herself'. Stripped of both a partner and the prospect of motherhood, her grief needed further time and support before she could resolve her career dilemma, which she saw as a choice between developing her fictional writing, and a complete change of career. Her concern to get on with her life alerted the counsellor to the possibility that she had not only insufficiently worked through her grief, but was also denying it. The counsellor felt that unless Joanna recognised what was happening to her she would continue to be blocked about her career, and suggested a referral to a bereavement counsellor.

Joanna's career issue was only the 'presenting problem', and, although its resolution was a priority, one career counselling meeting brought out more underlying problems, which needed attention first.

Other situations appropriate for referral
As indicated above, the need for referral may arise at any stage in the career counselling. Having completed the counselling, a referral may still be appropriate if, for example,

- career counselling has raised the client's awareness of the need for personal counselling about a major life issue from the past;
- the client needs specialist information which the career counsellor cannot provide (for example, about occupations, or educational grants).

The career counsellor needs a bank of referral resources: names, addresses and telephone numbers of local advisory bureaux and nationwide directories of counselling and psychotherapy services. One useful publication, regularly updated, is the British Association for Counselling's *Counselling and Psychotherapy Resources Directory*. It is particularly useful to build up a list of psychotherapists and counsellors who can be personally recommended.

Any referral should be made with care, especially referrals for personal counselling or psychotherapy. Such a suggestion can easily be interpreted by the client as a rejection, and may interfere with the rapport ('You think I'm crazy', or, 'Someone else can't help me – I've failed again'). The counsellor of course needs to be prepared to deal with the client's feelings during any discussion about referral. For a referral to be successful, the decision should be a joint one, and the reasons shared openly. It is quite reasonable, if appropriate, to suggest that the client can return for a further visit later on if it would be helpful. Making this offer can act as a useful 'bridge' for clients, even if they do not actually take up the offer.

In the case of referral for specialist or detailed information about careers it is useful to build up a list of personally known contacts in different occupations, who may act as 'human' sources of information for clients. This may be done by asking previous clients if they would be willing to be contacted. Addresses of professional associations should also be kept. See Appendix C for sources of careers information.

Advice giving: the dangers

It is sometimes very tempting to give advice to clients in career counselling. After all, they often ask for it! However, we believe that, as a general rule, career counsellors should avoid giving advice, for the reasons given in Box 7.2.

Box 7.2   *Disadvantages of advice giving in career counselling*

- It absolves clients from taking responsibility for their own decision making.
- The advice may be wrong for this person.
- Decisions arrived at through personal reflection and experience are more likely to stick and be satisfying.
- If the advice is wrong, the counsellor is likely to be blamed.
- In giving advice, it is tempting to offer a pet like or suggest avoiding a pet hate.

Even occupational information should be given with care (see also Chapter 5), as the following example shows:

It seemed very clear to the career counsellor that Jeremy's abilities, interests and personality indicated a certain group of occupations. Because of his training, he offered these suggestions merely as kite-fliers. However, the client avidly wrote them down.

What the career counsellor had overlooked was that testing had established that Jeremy was someone who needed structure and liked working with facts. He therefore regarded the counsellor's suggestions and the information he gathered before the next meeting as absolute facts, not as ideas on which to reflect. When he read the occupational information, Jeremy became downhearted when he found that nothing he read seemed 'practical'.

Perhaps a more 'intuitive' client would have treated the career counsellor's ideas as they were intended – as ideas. But perhaps not. The combination of the client's need for a solution together with the perceived expertise of the counsellor are often so strong that almost anything suggested can be taken 'on board'. It is not uncommon to hear, 'The counsellor said I should . . .'. On the other hand, if the counsellor suggests, 'Why don't you . . .', some clients will enjoy the opportunity to play the 'yes, but . . .' game (Berne, 1968).

Is it ever helpful to give advice?

Supposing the career counsellor feels convinced that the client is embarking on an inappropriate career choice? Does this constitute a case for intervention in order to save the client from what the counsellor thinks will be a dreadful mistake? Or even to protect those who will work with a client who subsequently might become embittered or even a danger? For example, an alcoholic who wants to become a firefighter; or a client who wants to become a counsellor, but is unwilling to deal with personal issues.

Some of the choices in this situation are as follows:

- Say nothing (silence may, however, be read as agreement).
- Allow clients to see the pointlessness of the decision through experience, for example, by applying for training or employment and being turned down.
- Point out lists of the skills and personal qualities required.
- Suggest that clients put themselves in the position of employers recruiting for the desired occupation.
- Give a direct opinion.

A time when it may be appropriate to give advice is at the stage when clients are relatively clear about their career direction and need 'technical' advice on job-hunting techniques (see p. 130).

Client resistance

It can be very frustrating when clients

- turn up late for appointments;
- miss appointments, usually giving a plausible excuse;
- fail to complete homework assignments;
- avoid keeping to the contract by, for example, continuing to expect the career counsellor to provide an 'answer'.

Such behaviour may be a covert expression of a client's feelings, particularly anger, and it may provide a useful 'message' about the client's problem, as in this case:

> Each appointment Roger was due to keep was fraught with confusion. On one occasion, he telephoned to say that his car had broken down. He asked whether it was worth coming as he would be half an hour late. On another occasion, he forgot entirely to attend.
>
> The 'truth' emerged when he was due to make a final appointment, and had to ask permission from his father, who was paying for the meetings.

In Roger's case, his father had wanted the career counselling to produce a particular result, and was only willing to finance the meetings if Roger used them in the way *he* wanted.

Although this is a relatively unusual example, some resistance or avoidance will tend to occur from time to time. The likelihood of such incidents and behaviour can be reduced by clear contracting. Where money is involved, payment at the first meeting for the whole programme, with a clear statement that missed appointments must be paid for, can test and increase commitment at the early stages of the career counselling. However, resistance cannot be eliminated and career counsellors might use such signs as a basis for:

- questioning clients' commitment to the career counselling;
- questioning clients' commitment to a career;
- exploring who else has a vested interest in the outcome of the career counselling;
- challenging clients to make their covert anger more overt (and therefore less likely to be acted out in the client–counsellor relationship);
- considering whether career counselling is not meeting the client's real needs.

Working with 'significant others'

Although the career counsellor is always responsible to the individual client, there will be occasions when another party is involved in, or will be affected by, the client's decision-making process.

This might be a parent, partner, spouse, friend or relation. In the case of a referral, it may include employers, social workers, doctors and psychotherapists. (See Chapter 3 for a discussion of the implications of third-party referrals.)

In some cases, the client will have shared the tape recording made in an earlier meeting (see Chapter 5, p. 85) with his or her parents or partner. Parents can be a big help to the career counselling process, because of their concern for and knowledge of their son or daughter. For the same reasons, they can be a hindrance, frequently wishing to further their own agendas for their children, for example, by pressurising them to:

- follow the family line (for example, go to Cambridge);
- do the opposite of what they did (for example, don't run a business);
- take a particular course (for example, science or engineering, which is seen as vocational and more likely to lead to a secure job).

Joint meetings can air any conflicts between the young person and his or her parents, allowing their respective thoughts and feelings to be addressed in ways not done previously:

> Alan and his mother were over half an hour early for the final meeting. When the career counsellor went into the waiting room, he found that Alan and his mum were already in the middle of a lively conversation about his career, and were addressing issues they had not done before.

On other occasions, however, it can be hard to avoid being pulled into the family 'system' and taking sides:

> The career counsellor was known to Emma, who had contacted the career counselling service with a view to sponsoring her nephew Jamie. In the first meeting with Jamie, it became apparent that he had resolved to follow a particular career, and wanted to use the time to explore ways in which he could build on his strengths and minimise the impact of his weaknesses within his chosen career. However, in the final

meeting, Emma wanted to know why the career counselling had not assessed Jamie's suitability for different careers. She was convinced that his choice of occupation was utterly wrong. The career counsellor felt pulled in different directions but attempted to enable Emma and Jamie to hear each other's points of view. This was virtually in the form of 'interpretations' of what one was saying to or about the other.

Third parties can also become involved in the career counselling indirectly. One example was a married man who was 'encouraged' by his wife to come. It proved productive to look at his feelings about her desires for his career as part of the process of considering what career might be appropriate for him. Another example was a man of 24 whose father paid for the career counselling, and was disappointed that the counsellor had not recommended a career more in line with his own expectations. In fact, the client had seemed happy with the outcome of the work, but, because the career counsellor had not taken sufficient account of the influence of the father over his son, the apparently good result was undermined.

Equal opportunity issues in career counselling

As we mentioned in Chapter 2, factors such as race, class, gender and disability are important in determining an individual's career development, and career counsellors need to have an understanding of equal opportunities issues in order to practise career counselling in a way which counters the effects of oppression on people from 'minority' groups.

Ideas, attitudes and assumptions about people who do not conform to the 'norm' of the 'majority' culture can operate against the interests of people from certain groups, so that they have unequal life chances. They do not have equal access to educational and employment opportunities. They face an extra task of coming to terms with what the issue of being black, female or working class means in terms of barriers and obstacles to their career development, as the following case study shows:

Chris was 27 and approached a career counsellor to discuss his future prospects. He was born and educated in Britain but his parents had emigrated from the Caribbean. His school encouraged him to achieve on the sports field but not academically. He left with only two GCEs, but went on to study part-time at college whilst supporting himself financially through working as a fast-food assistant. He eventually achieved two good A-level passes and tried for a better job. After many unsuccessful attempts to get an office job, he decided to apply for a business studies degree course. On graduating, he was unable to find a job in the commercial sector, but eventually found work as a clerical assistant with the local council. After two years, he was promoted to a supervisory role. Still trying to better himself, he had in the mean time begun to study for a postgraduate management qualification in his own time. He had not told his manager about his studies, and had just been sent on a low-level supervisory training course.

In the career counselling, it emerged that, understandably, Chris was diffident about 'blowing his own trumpet' regarding his management studies, for fear that his expertise would yet again be rejected. It was important for the career counsellor to validate Chris's feelings of frustration at all the barriers he had encountered. However, the career counselling moved on to a pragmatic level, helping Chris to develop his self-presentation and assertiveness skills. Later, Chris negotiated with his manager and was given projects which made use of the management skills he had acquired.

Here are a number of guidelines to enhance professional practice.

- Develop your understanding of how society is structured and how the 'system' operates in relation to education and employment opportunities for certain groups.
- Monitor how, for example, your own gender, cultural or racial background and social class affect your work with clients. Examine honestly your prejudices and conditioning. Stereotypes, for example that Asians are good with figures or that gay men are effeminate, may prevent the unaware counsellor from seeing the individual objectively, and from listening and empathising effectively across class, race, gender, religious, age and any other boundaries.
- Accept that the anger and frustration that clients from groups which face discrimination feel is legitimate, and not due to an inner psychopathology.
- Be aware that if people are assailed from birth with messages that they are second class, their self-esteem may not be first class. Offer help such as confidence-building and assertiveness techniques to challenge discrimination, or refer the client to sources of such support.

- Remember that many people from minority groups will have experienced a disproportionate number of rejections when applying for jobs. In particular, it is likely that black clients will have encountered racism when dealing with predominately white organisations.
- Encourage clients to examine the full spectrum of career options. Women may have been brainwashed into considering either the traditional 'wife and mother' role, or a limited range of gender-stereotyped occupations. Black people may have less access to informal sources of occupational information in their own networks, and may need more help than white people in locating sources of information (see Chapter 5).
- When working with women, avoid perpetuating the 'having a career or a family' dichotomy. For most women who want children, the issue is no longer whether to do both, but how to do both.
- Ensure that you properly understand and value qualifications that have been obtained elsewhere. In England, for example, one form that ethnocentricism (the belief in the supremacy of one's own culture) takes is assumptions and views that English qualifications are superior to qualifications gained elsewhere – in Nigeria, Ireland, Scotland, India, Jamaica or France, for instance.
- In the case of a client with limited written or spoken English, don't assume that this is evidence of limited ability. It is likely to be the consequence of a lack of relevant opportunities to learn English. Be aware that in a cross-cultural situation, both verbal and non-verbal communication may be more open to misinterpretation.

For an in-depth discussion of counselling people from minority groups, see Sue and Sue (1990).

Skills and knowledge valuable to career counsellors

It is assumed throughout this book that all practising career counsellors will have developed, through a combination of training and experience, the basic skills of counselling. Box 7.3 lists some of the skills, attitudes and behaviours which constitute the basis of all good counselling practice. The reader can discover more about these basic skills in Egan (1990) or Inskipp (1988).

However, in the practice of career counselling, a number of areas of specialist skill and knowledge are required in addition to these.

Box 7.3   *Basic counselling skills, attitudes and behaviours*

- Ensuring that the physical setting is conducive to establishing trust;
- Making clear contracts with clients;
- Being aware of what interferes with effective listening;
- Respecting clients and accepting their social contexts;
- Using responding skills (including reflecting, clarifying, probing, summarising and open-question techniques) in an appropriate manner;
- Using challenging and confronting skills, where appropriate;
- Using silence appropriately;
- Being aware and having experience of at least one model of counselling;
- Ensuring that proper and adequate supervision is received.

Knowledge of factors relevant to career management
Career counsellors should have at least a general knowledge of careers, for example of job families and levels (see pp. 89–90). In addition to this framework of occupations, career counsellors need a knowledge of important issues in career management, so that the relevant ones can be addressed with clients. Their discussion may enable clients to plan the management of their careers differently. For example, it is not uncommon for clients to say that they had never thought of the idea of taking two part-time jobs, instead of one full-time occupation; or that other people had similar, unconventional career patterns to themselves and had survived! Box 7.4 lists some career management issues which are described in more detail in this section.

Box 7.4   *Career management concerns*

- Patterns of career development may be vertical, horizontal or cyclical.
- Alternatives to full-time employment are possible.
- Some techniques can assist career management (for example a 'stepping stone' job).
- Certain needs, values and interests *drive* people in their careers.
- People choose not only a set of tasks in a career, but also a social and cultural context.
- Self-managed career development is more the norm today.

Career patterns

Many people who were brought up in times of full employment expected a full-time job (35 hours a week) from the end of their schooling, college or apprenticeship days until retirement. If they are not able to conform to this expected pattern of behaviour, they feel they have failed.

Two recessions in ten years, plus increasing demand for specialist skills, an ageing population and a greater number of women taking their careers outside the home more seriously have provided the impetus for many changes in the kinds of work opportunity available and the willingness to work in non-traditional ways. Changes in how organisations are structured are revolutionising attitudes to expected patterns of career development, such as through promotions and upward mobility (Mael, 1991).

People who have followed a less traditional career pattern can no longer be seen by anyone, especially career counsellors, as failures. In addition to the vertical, upwardly mobile pattern of career development is the 'horizontal' pattern. As the name suggests, movement is across levels, rather than up the organisational hierarchy. For example, an industrial chemist who does not want or is not seen by his or her employer as able to become a manager may transfer to a new project. Or a systems analyst might move from a back-room analytical role to a more customer-contact one. Such development can be seen as a gradual process of learning, and is compatible with the demands of many large employing organisations today who need to have a staff able to adapt to their ever-changing requirements.

It is quite likely that career counsellors will meet people who have jumped around from one occupation to another, without ever seeming to settle down. They come for career counselling, more confused by the disapproval of parents and the felt need for a consistent curriculum vitae, than by any sense of their own that they have failed or been in unsuitable work. Perhaps they see their lives more as a whole than in terms of occupational success alone. The work of the career counsellor may need first to focus on re-affirming such clients' sense of self-worth by validation of their 'cyclical' pattern of experience before planning for the future. There is, for example, a great deal of experience and skill that someone who has been a nurse, secretary, computer programmer, caterer and counsellor can offer, not least experience of many different organisational settings, styles of management and the skill of establishing relationships quickly.

For obvious reasons, the career patterns of women with children often appear more 'untidy' than those of men, and may involve a fresh start after child-rearing (see Lemmer, 1991). It is important not to judge women's careers by male norms.

Knowledge of alternatives to traditional full-time employment

In order to assist clients to develop occupational ideas, career counsellors should know, or have access to knowledge, about alternatives to the conventional idea of a career. The reality is that fewer 'jobs for life' are available, and clients may still harbour hopes based on outmoded values and expectations.

By referring to the existence of alternative possibilities along with more conventional ideas, the career counsellor can validate as a viable alternative an idea which may be totally new to a client. Some possible alternatives to a full-time 'job for life', including part-time work, self-employment, franchising, cooperatives and temporary, contractual or freelance work are discussed in Nathan and Syrett (1983).

The idea that a part-time position might allow a client to develop a new skill or try out a business idea without full commitment can be very liberating for a client who may have become stuck in believing that choices have to be made in the ways they always were.

The advantages of part-time work have now been recognised by both employers and individuals, and include the following:

- It gives paid experience (usable on a CV).
- It can provide a reference.
- It enables social contact to be continued.
- It can help to ease the change from full-time to self-employment.
- It provides continued activity and structure to the day.
- It may provide some of the finance required for part-time education or training.
- It may help to finance the setting up of a small business.
- It may lead to a full-time job.

Britain has the highest number of part-time employees (one in five) in Europe. In March 1988 the *Labour Market Quarterly Report*, published by the Manpower Services Commission, claimed that the majority of new jobs created up until the mid-1990s would be for part-timers. One example of an employer which has taken part-time employment seriously is Sainsbury's which, in mid-1989, took on about 230 part-time managers, with equivalent benefits and pension rights to full-timers.

'Stepping stones' – a technique of career development

Clients often come looking for the ideal job or career, partly as an antidote to their present confusion. The idealised version of their career will, they think, somehow remove all their misery. A useful point of focus for career counsellors is to be aware of clients' relationship with this ideal. It may be very important for the client to maintain it as an ideal: at least, the client believes, there is still something good that could be possible. But once the counsellor attempts to break down the dream idea into some realistic component parts, strong resistance may be shown by the client. The 'tea shoppe' in the country, the B.&B. or the wine bar idea may, however, provide the basis for developing a more workable and realistic proposition.

Once a more reasonable aim has been agreed, it is then possible to discuss with clients appropriate ways of getting there. Disappointing though it may be for clients, the next 'job' may not be *the* one. It is at this point that the career counsellor can introduce the idea of stepping stones as a legitimate and normal way of making progress towards an occupational goal. For example, the client considering starting a bed and breakfast establishment may decide to work for a while in a small hotel in the location under consideration. A social worker wanting to become a trainer may decide to teach social work for a couple of years and take the qualifications of the Institute of Training and Development before applying for training jobs. Someone wanting to enter the field of graduate recruitment may work first in a Youth Training Scheme, gaining knowledge and experience of working with young people.

Appraising clients of such possibilities can reduce their sense of urgency that the next job *must* be the right one. This applies equally to clients who feel they *must* leave their current employer, possibly because of a personality clash with a supervisor or colleague or because of a disillusionment with their lack of progress. It may be possible to defuse clients' sense of urgency by describing the technique of stepping stones as a valid and viable way out of the organisation and, equally important, as an undoubtedly easier way of changing careers than approaching the job market directly. An example would be a salesperson who wants to move into marketing having a better chance on the open job market if he or she first gains marketing experience.

Knowledge of career drivers

A career driver is an 'inner force which determines what you want and what you need from your working life' (Francis, 1985). The idea of career drivers comes from the work of Schein (1978). If career counsellors have knowledge of the main drivers, they will be better able to assist clients to address some key questions. For example, a technically trained client – an engineer – may be considering the possibility of becoming a manager in order to 'get on'. A discussion of the career drivers described in Box 7.5 may help to put the client's motives and values in perspective. A questionnaire which provides a structured basis for discussing career drivers is detailed in Francis (1985).

Box 7.5   *Career drivers*

- *Material rewards* – seeking possession, wealth and a high standard of living.
- *Power and influence* – seeking to be in control of people and resources.
- *Search for meaning* – seeking to do things believed to be valuable for their own sake.
- *Expertise* – seeking a high level of accomplishment in a specialised field.
- *Creativity* – seeking to innovate and be identified with original input.
- *Affiliation* – seeking nourishing relationships with others at work.
- *Autonomy* – seeking to be independent and make key decisions for oneself.
- *Status* – seeking to be recognised, admired and respected by the community at large.
- *Security* – seeking a solid and predictable future.

Social and cultural aspects of occupational choice and satisfaction

It is fashionable to talk of *transferable skills* – the helpful idea that skills may be transferred from one occupational environment to another (for example teachers can take their 'persuading' skills to a selling career). However, there are factors other than the application of skills to tasks which contribute to occupational satisfaction and success. Of particular importance is the degree to which a person can adapt to the demands of an organisation's culture, that is its values, expectations, systems of operation and reward, and its people. Some specific considerations include:

- size of organisation;
- private or public sector;
- centralised or decentralised control;
- security of employment provided;
- nature of the product or service.

Indeed, clients may sometimes be choosing organisational type, colleagues and a boss as much as the type of work.

Awareness of the principles of self-managed career development

Career counsellors should be aware of the lead being given by some large organisations in encouraging self-managed career development (see Jackson, 1990) and the ways in which clients can manage their careers once the career counselling sessions are finished.

In addition to continued self-assessment (hopefully a by-product of the career counselling), one important career management skill is knowing ways of evaluating jobs and organisations (London and Stumpf, 1982). Another is the knowledge of organisations' selection and recruitment practices, and using effective self-promotion techniques.

Knowledge of job-hunting skills and techniques

It is important for career counsellors to provide assistance with, at least, the basics of job-hunting skills. This means that familiarity should be gained with:

- the principles of writing curricula vitae;
- the major methods and sources of job finding;
- techniques of completing application forms and writing letters of application;
- effective approaches to job interviews.

The career counsellor may have the resources to provide such assistance or may refer to a Job Centre, government-sponsored programme or in-house course, if working in a college or large organisation.

Discussion on the best approach to job hunting is of course most relevant when clients are relatively clear about their career direction. At this point, it is appropriate for the career counsellor to put on more of an 'expert' hat, and give advice and information to clients (see p. 118 on the disadvantages of advice giving).

Job applications should make use of all the techniques available, including the use of personal contacts, networking, information interviewing and writing speculative letters, as well as the more traditional (but increasingly less effective) ways of applying to advertised vacancies and using recruitment consultants. See Floyed and Nathan (1991) for further discussion on effective techniques of job hunting.

Summary

In this chapter we have considered some of the important issues career counsellors may face in the course of their work. The questions addressed included:

- What are the boundaries between career and personal counselling?
- When is referral appropriate?
- Is it ever appropriate to give advice?
- How can third parties affect the career counselling?
- How can career counsellors work best with people from certain minority groups?
- What are the particular skills, knowledge and other qualities required by career counsellors?

In the final chapter we look at self-management for the career counsellor.

8
Self-Management for Career Counsellors

In this chapter the monitoring and evaluation of practice, together with support and professional development for career counsellors, is addressed. The purpose of effective self-management in career counselling is similar to its purpose in other counselling contexts – to ensure that clients receive the best possible attention.

Everyone has their own individual flaws and blocks, and career counsellors should receive appropriate individual or group supervision to ensure that these do not adversely affect their work. Together with continued learning opportunities (perhaps through training and attending professional meetings), supervision is important for the career counsellor's development. Career counselling is a demanding occupation and counsellors need to look after themselves between, during and after sessions with clients. Good support is necessary from colleagues, to offload, to share areas of common interest, to pool knowledge and to reduce isolation. In addition, supervision plays a supportive role for the counsellor.

Constant self-monitoring and examination of the career counsellor's own work, which may usefully draw on feedback from clients, is also important.

Monitoring and evaluating practice
Evaluating career counselling is a complex process because the results are not easily quantifiable. Killeen and Kidd (1991) have reviewed a number of research studies examining the success of guidance (including counselling). The studies, mainly conducted on work with young people, showed outcomes such as increased certainty of a decision, improved decision-making skills and increased exploration of options.

What is the 'product' of successful career counselling? Some form of change. As we saw in the previous chapter, changes may be external (for example, a new job) or internal (new confidence, for instance). The following client did not get a new job but considered that his career counselling was very successful:

Eric was a schoolteacher in his forties who came to career

counselling to find out whether his dissatisfaction was due to his unsuitability for teaching. After several meetings and doing a number of tests, questionnaires and exercises, he came to the conclusion that teaching was basically the right area for him. Testing showed him to be rather passive, and part of his action plan at the final meeting was to go on an assertiveness course. He found this very useful, and a year later he reported that he was feeling more self-confident and settled. A career change was not the real solution; knowing his strengths and working on his weaknesses was.

Changes may not be easily attributable to the career counselling; a combination of factors, including the counselling, may lead to change. Although outcomes for the client may throw some light on the question, 'Was the counselling successful?', we cannot evaluate the career counselling process solely on the basis of what the client has or has not been able to do because of the influence of other factors such as the economic situation and unpredictable life events. When considering criteria for what constitutes success, we believe that what is important is not whether clients have reached a destination, but that they end by feeling in a position to continue the journey:

> Career counselling gave me the self-confidence to recognise that I had a lot to offer, which helped me to decide to do what I really wanted. This was not decided at the sessions, but was an ongoing process that stemmed from them.

Ultimately, the career counsellor can only really rely on his or her honest self-evaluation. This may be done in various ways:

- alone, by reflecting on your own practice, reviewing client notes and considering any evaluative feedback the client may have provided;
- with the help of peers, informally, in team meetings or group supervision;
- with the help of the manager of the service;
- with the help of an external supervisor;
- through courses and professional meetings.

Using some of the questions listed in Box 8.1 may be useful in the process of self-evaluation.

Box 8.1   *Questions for self-evaluation*

Did I provide the best conditions for the client to pursue his or her career counselling journey?

Did I avoid giving advice, allowing this client to move in his or her own direction?

Did I work from the client's own starting point, taking into account individual circumstances and needs?

Did I avoid stereotyping this client, that is not making assumptions on the basis of race, gender, social class, age, culture, sexuality, disability?

(If testing was used) Did I offer feedback in a way which made the most positive use of the test information?

(If exercises were used) Did I incorporate the most appropriate exercises in the most helpful way?

What emotions were triggered off in me, and what was their source?

What am I pleased about with this piece of work?

What would I have done differently?

What did I learn from this client?

Evaluation by clients

Although evaluative feedback from clients is one source of information which the counsellor can consider in the process of self-evaluation, it is important not to rely on it as the only source. Feedback from clients is inevitably subjective. If life has improved, there may be a tendency to evaluate the career counselling positively. If life has not improved, one way of dealing with feelings of inadequacy is to project them on to the career counselling. Clients who have unresolved destructive and critical patterns of behaviour are likely to behave in that way with a feedback form too.

Evaluation should be a positive experience for the client. Inviting the client to evaluate the career counselling received helps to clarify and reinforce what has been gained, and keeps the momentum going (see pp. 112–13).

Some clients (especially those with a clearly delineated objective) may have achieved everything they wanted from career counselling by the end of the final meeting:

Joseph (see p. 92) had wanted to change career direction for a long time and had been through a careful process of considering his options before he came for career counselling. He wanted to assess his suitability for retraining as a physiotherapist. Understandably, he wanted to satisfy himself that he had the required attributes before he invested time and money in training. At the final meeting, Joseph was satisfied that he had achieved his objective, and went ahead with confidence to apply for courses in physiotherapy.

Such a totally successful outcome is rare. Many clients are at the very beginning of a longer process of continued self-understanding and exploration of options:

Sylvia was 25 and had been unemployed for six months when she came for career counselling. Her education had been greatly disrupted by the death of her mother during her adolescence, and Sylvia's examination achievements were poor. She was also in the process of recovering from injuries sustained in a car accident and was feeling quite lonely and isolated. Career counselling showed her that she had far greater intellectual capabilities than she had expected. By the final meeting, she had decided that she would like to pursue her studies as a mature student, with a view to developing a career in the scientific or medical field. Her action plan covered a number of points, including researching different careers and courses, enquiring about her grant situation, building up her physical fitness, and developing new friendships.

When is the best time to evaluate?
Career counselling clients are in a process of transition, so changes may take place over an extended period of time in quite a subtle way. Immediately afterwards, a client may not see the benefit, and may complain that they still don't know what to do, as the following case study demonstrates:

Tracey was asked to evaluate the career counselling shortly after her final meeting. At this meeting, the counsellor had reiterated the importance of making her own decision about what to do. The questionnaire asked about her expectations and the extent to which they had been met. She replied that she had wanted the counselling to point her in the 'right direction', and match her skills and qualities to suitable careers. She felt disappointed that this had not happened and felt she had been 'left up in the air'. She was clearly sceptical about the value of the counselling. A year later she was sent a follow-up questionnaire. She now felt that the career counselling had made 'a lot of difference' for her. She said that her objective of narrowing down her choice of career had been 'completely achieved'. She writes: 'the counselling takes time to sink in. . .without realising it, I am in actual fact doing what was shown to be suited to me.' On all the job satisfaction criteria which the career counselling had helped her to identify, the job she was doing was giving her a high degree of satisfaction.

For people making complex changes in their lives, even a year is quite a short time scale.

Some useful questions which can be asked on an evaluation form are listed in Box 8.2.

Box 8.2   *Client evaluation form*

What were your expectations of career counselling?
To what extent have they been met?
What in particular did you gain from career counselling?
How could you have gained more from career counselling?
Would you recommend the service to others?

Indicate the extent to which you agree or disagree with the following statements:
  Career counselling helped me to:

- feel more confident;
- think more clearly about what I want from work;
- understand my strengths and weaknesses;
- decide on a plan for the future;
- narrow down my choice of occupation;
- tie up information about myself to possible jobs.

At a one-year follow-up, clients can be asked for details of their current job, employer, main work functions and work responsibilities.

Our own evaluation practice is as follows. At the final meeting we invite clients to evaluate the career counselling in relation to their original objectives, that is those agreed at the earlier contracting stage. When clients receive a summary (soon after the final meeting), we also send a feedback form. A year later we invite clients to evaluate the career counselling again, to assess the longer-term impact, so that we can see what people are doing differently in their lives. We also note the source of referrals and monitor how many come from personal recommendation of past clients, as this is an expression of how past clients value the service. We record the information systematically, and analyse it, noting any unintended or unexpected outcomes or spin-offs. We identify and immediately act upon any request for further help from the client.

Personal and professional development

The process of monitoring and evaluating the career counselling provided will enable career counsellors to identify their personal and professional development needs. There are a number of ways of meeting these needs:

- Further development of generic counselling skills, by attending, for example, short workshops or extended courses.
- Further development of specialist career counselling skills.
- Attending professional meetings (for example, British Association for Counselling, British Psychological Society, Institute of Careers Guidance, Institute of Personnel Management's Outplacement Forum).
- Attending career conferences (for example, arranged by CRAC, the Careers Research Advisory Centre).
- Reading appropriate books and academic journals (see Appendix C and Appendix G for information).
- Obtaining counselling or therapy to work through personal issues. (For career counsellors with issues relating to their own career satisfaction, success and achievement, obtaining career counselling may be appropriate.)
- Occupational visits.
- Attending college open days.
- Supervision.

Supervision

Hess's (1980) commonly used definition of supervision describes it as an 'interpersonal interaction with the general goal that one person, the supervisor, meets with another, the supervisee, in an effort to make the latter more effective in helping people'. Supervision is a regular, structured opportunity for the career counsellor to examine his or her work. It has a threefold function of enabling the practitioner to learn and develop competence, to obtain support and encouragement, and to ensure good professional standards of practice. Proctor (1988) uses the terms 'formative', 'restorative' and 'normative' respectively for these functions.

Although some career counsellors will have supervision with their manager, we believe that this is no substitute for non-managerial supervision. Whether practised in groups or one to one, supervision is as essential a requirement for the career counsellor as it is for any other counsellor, as outlined in the British Association for Counselling's *Code of Ethics* (1990).

Supervision can help career counsellors to obtain new perspectives, to assess the nature of the client's problem, to discuss the management of difficult cases, to assist in test interpretation, and to deal with feelings in relation to the client. In particular, it can help the counsellor to deal with the pressures of 'getting a result'. A client's anxiety for a solution is very contagious, and career counsellors often 'catch' it.

We believe that one-to-one supervision is especially appropriate at the stage when a career counsellor is 'learning the ropes'. If sessions with the client are tape-recorded (with the client's permission), the supervisor can listen to recordings and then discuss the work with the counsellor.

For the experienced career counsellor, we have found group approaches to supervision to be more beneficial, with counsellors taking turns to discuss their work. Such groups can be facilitated or peer-led. Although time management can be an issue, within a group there is a wider range of expertise to bring to bear on the career counsellor/client relationship being discussed. A co-counselling model where two counsellors 'exchange' supervision, taking turns to act as supervisor and supervisee, may also be appropriate for more experienced counsellors.

Hawkins and Shohet (1989) have written comprehensively about models and processes of supervision in the helping professions generally, and the interested reader is referred to their book.

Case study   A group of three experienced career counsellors meet for 1½ hours every fortnight for supervision. At one of their meetings, the following issues were discussed:

> Josephine described an initial meeting she had had with a highly disturbed and very angry client. She was able to offload her feelings of fear, and obtain reassurance from her colleagues about the course of action she had adopted, which was to recommend that the client see his doctor about being referred for psychotherapy.

Lorraine discussed her difficulties in counselling a client who had been sacked from his last three jobs. He had a history of being severely bullied at school. She realised through examining some feelings of revulsion towards him that some memories of her own difficulties at school were being triggered off. She also sought her colleagues' help in interpreting the meaning of the personality profile of one of her clients.

Doug brought two recent cases where both clients expected that he would have 'all the answers'. Just by talking through the pressures he felt, he realised that these clients were looking to him as a father figure, and he recognised the part in him which enjoyed being put on a pedestal.

Self-management between and during sessions

Career counsellors need to be in as good mental and physical condition for the first and last clients of the day. One reason why people enter the caring professions is that they enjoy helping others. It is therefore hard to say no when asked for help, but responding to caseload pressures by squeezing in more and more clients for even shorter appointments is a rapid route to, at best, inefficiency and, at worst, burnout. Often, counsellors do not realise the long-term damage they might be causing themselves and, in turn, that they will be providing a less professional service to clients. In a discussion of factors contributing to burnout, Nelson-Jones (1991) outlines the following causes:

perfectionism;
undue pessimism;
unrealistically high goals;
undue need for approval;
inability to set limits on workload;
poor time management;
insufficient recreational outlets;
poor skills at looking after health and physical fitness.

Although Nelson-Jones was referring to people who run lifeskills training groups, these causes are equally pertinent to career counsellors.

Ways in which career counsellors can look after themselves between and during sessions include:

– having at least a half-hour gap between clients, to allow for note taking, preparation and a non-counselling-related activity;

- using the break between clients to attend to something quite different (for example taking a walk, having a cup of tea or a chat with a colleague, doing a tension-reduction exercise);[1]
- seeing no more than three or four clients a day, at 1½ hours each;
- not seeing clients all five days per week;
- asking a colleague for some counselling time if left with any distressing feelings from a previous client; being prepared to share negative feelings – for example, of failure or power-lessness;
- using the counselling skills of challenging and immediacy (see Egan, 1990) within sessions to avoid being trapped into destructive transference and countertransference problems;
- having an icon within sight which evokes feelings of peace or serenity, for example, a photograph, picture, flower or favourite saying.

Another way in which career counsellors in some (but not all) settings can look after themselves is by not feeling obliged to take on all clients who are requesting career counselling. A career counsellor may not feel able or willing to take on a particular client, perhaps because the client and counsellor hold such opposing values that the counsellor finds it impossible to listen to and empathise with the client. It is worth addressing this dilemma before becoming committed to a series of unproductive and draining meetings. It might be feasible to build into a contract some kind of 'opt out' clause, so that either client or counsellor can withdraw after the first meeting if either feels unable to work with the other.

Above all, it is important to avoid becoming trapped into colluding with a client's desire for you to provide an answer. As we have seen, this is especially prevalent in career counselling. It is not the career counsellor's responsibility to ensure that the client gets a job. A client may have a legitimate need to find a job quickly to pay for essential living requirements, but this should not detract from the goals of career counselling established at the beginning of the contract. These will probably focus on resolving some of the pressures brought about by the need to earn a living in relation to the personal desire for a satisfying occupation. Such a resolution may not be achieved within the counselling meetings, but it may evolve when a client has had a chance to test out some of the ideas developed in the career counselling.

1. One tension-reduction exercise is to completely flop in your chair, allowing all your muscles to collapse as you reach for the floor. Then, after about one minute, slowly revert to your sitting position.

Appendix A
Guidelines for Tests

These 'guidelines' can be given to clients at the end of the first meeting, where aptitude or ability tests are to be given.

Testing is a part of the process of career counselling which provides helpful information about you by making an objective assessment of your abilities, interests and personality. Tests are objective; they have been given to thousands of people. This ensures that the information they provide is useful and valid.

Tests play an important part, but need to be seen in the whole context of career counselling. They are just one source of information about you, and their results will not be accepted blindly at face value. Although objective, they can be affected by your attitude to testing, your feeling on the day, and anxiety.

Your counsellor will help you to understand how such factors may have affected you, when you discuss the results together.

Test administration

The tests may seem rather like an exam because they are accurately timed and carried out under fixed conditions and because there may be another person or other people doing the tests at the same time as you. *However*, they are not competitive, and are purely a way of finding out about you.

The testing meeting lasts from 4½ to 5 hours and is broken down into a number of shorter tests, with a break in the middle. Most of the time will be spent on aptitude tests, but there will be a number of short, untimed questionnaires to fill out as well.

Appendix B
Action Plan

Be clear about your goal (where you want to be).

1. My goal is:

Consider the gap between where you are now and where you want to be, and the steps you will need to take to bridge the gap. List the most useful 'action steps' (what you need to do to achieve your goal) without worrying about their sequence. Be very specific about what each step involves.

2. My action steps are:

3. Number the action steps in a logical sequence

4. Write down your plan:

    Tomorrow I will . . .
    Over the next week I will . . .
    Over the next month I will . . .
    Over the next three months I will . . .
    Over the next six months I will . . .

5. Decide when you will review progress:

    My review date will be . . .

Appendix C
Sources of Occupational Information

Libraries

Public libraries are a useful starting point for information about courses and careers. Two specialist libraries which stock relevant material are:

The City Business Library, 1 Brewers' Hall Garden, London EC2V 5BX (Tel. 071–638 8215)

Science Reference and Information Service (British Library), 25 Southampton Buildings, Chancery Lane, London WC2A 1AW (Tel. 071–323 7494/6)

Careers service

Usually part of the local education authority, careers services provide information about careers, education and training. They specialise in careers information for young people, but many offer a service to adults too.

Educational guidance services

Educational guidance services provide information about learning opportunities to the general public. A directory of services, compiled by Jane Barrett, is available from the Further Education Unit, 2 Orange Street, London WC2H 7WE.

Computerised databases

There is a trend for computerised occupational information to be publicly available, for example, in libraries. Local Training and Enterprise Councils are establishing a network of Training Access Points (TAPs) which provide accessible computerised information about learning opportunities to members of the public. For a survey of careers software, see Offer (1991a).

Professional bodies

A large number of professional bodies and trade associations produce careers information, much of which is provided at little or no cost to the enquirer. The CIOLA directory (Shepherd, 1991) provides a comprehensive listing of these organisations.

Reference books

For career counsellors, some of the most useful publications for reference include:

Occupations, Careers and Occupational Information Centre (annual).
Jobfile, Hodder & Stoughton (annual).
British Qualifications, Kogan Page (annual).
Second Chances, Careers and Occupational Information Centre (annual).
Kemp, D. and Kemp, F., *The Mid-Career Action Guide: a Practical Guide to Mid-career Change*, Kogan Page, 1991.
Alston, A. and Daniel, A., *The Penguin Careers Guide*, Penguin, 1992.

Guides to specific careers

A number of publishers produce guides to specific careers, each of which describes the nature of the work, together with details of entry and training.

Recruitment agencies

For details of recruitment agencies, consult the *Yearbook of Recruitment and Employment Services*, available from FRES, 36 Mortimer Street, London W1N 7RB (Tel. 071–323 4300). *The Personnel Manager's Yearbook* (AP Services, annual publication) contains a modest listing. The City Polytechnic Careers Service, 31 Jewry Street, London EC3N 2EY, has produced a survey of recruitment agencies in the London area.

Appendix D
The Use of Computers in Career Counselling

Software is becoming increasingly sophisticated, and a number of programs are available for career counselling purposes. Most can be used by clients with little or no assistance from the career counsellor, and they can be a useful additional tool in the career counsellor's kit. Three main types of software are used in career counselling:

Databases These provide accurate, up-to-date information about career/job opportunities, together with some means of retrieving information according to certain criteria, for example jobs in a particular career area (such as work with children), or careers requiring a degree-level qualification. The most widely used programs at the time of writing are Jobfile Explorer, Computer Signposts and MicroDOORS/OpenDOORS (which covers over 1,000 job titles).

'Matching' programs These assess individuals on the basis of, for example, interests, skills, personality and values, and then generate job possibilities which match the individual. We feel that these systems are simplistic and, to date, fail to address the complexity of the factors that affect career decision making. However, provided the client understands their limitations, they can be useful in generating job ideas for further consideration. Two popular programs for adults are Careerbuilder and Cascaid HE (for graduates).

Computerised tests A number of standardised interest inventories, personality questionnaires and aptitude test batteries are available on computer. Computerised psychometric tests have the obvious advantage of standardised administration, together with speed and accuracy in marking. As with pencil-and-paper forms of psycho-metric tests, the purchase of many of these instruments is restricted to people with psychology degrees and/or appropriate training.

In addition, we will mention two important databases which cover learning opportunities:

The Educational Counselling and Credit Transfer Information Service provides computerised information on further and higher education courses. This database is available on subscription from ECCTIS, Fulton House, Jessop Avenue, Cheltenham, Glos GL50 3SH.

The NVQ Database provides comprehensive information about the new system of National Vocational Qualifications. It can be used at any local TEC (Training and Enterprise Council).

For detailed software reviews see Offer (1991a), and for a discussion of the use of computers in careers work, see Offer (1991b).

Appendix E
Self-help Workbooks

These publications contain exercises that can be used by individuals who want to further their career development. To gain maximum benefit from them, some discussion of the exercises is necessary, so workbooks are best used as an adjunct to career counselling.

General

Bolles, R.N. (1991) *What Colour is Your Parachute?* Berkeley, CA: Ten Speed Press.

Dail, H.L. (1989) *The Lotus and the Pool: How to Create Your Own Career*, Boston, MA: Shambhala Publications.

Hopson, B. and Scally, M., (1989) *Build Your own Rainbow: a Workbook for Career and Life Management*, Leeds: Lifeskills Associates.

Nathan, R. and Floyed, J. (1991) *The CCS Self Assessment Manual*. London: Career Counselling Services.

For people in mid-life

Smith, M. (1989) *The Best is Yet to Come: a Workbook for the Middle Years*, Sheffield: Lifeskills Associates.

For women

Willis, L. and Daisley, J. (1990) *Springboard: Women's Development Workbook*. Stroud, Glos.: Hawthorn Press.

For young people

Crowley, A. (1989) *Breakout: Books 1–3*. Cambridge: Careers Research and Advisory Centre.

For managers

Francis, D. (1985) *Managing Your Own Career*. London: Collins.

Appendix F
Training Courses

The most relevant professional preparation for the career counsellor is training and experience which leads to membership of (or accreditation by) the following organisations:

BAC (British Association for Counselling);
BPS (British Psychological Society);
ICG (Institute of Careers Guidance);
IPM (Institute of Personnel Management);
ITD (Institute of Training and Development).

A new scheme for qualifications in the guidance and counselling field is currently being developed within the framework of National Vocational Qualifications (NVQ). See Appendix H for addresses.

Appendix G
Relevant Journals

British Journal of Guidance and Counselling. Cambridge: CRAC.

Career Development Quarterly. Alexandria, VA: AACD.

Counselling. Rugby: BAC.

Counselling News. London: Central Magazines.

The Counselling Psychologist. Newbury Park: Sage.

HR Magazine. (USA).

Human Resources. London: Portman Press.

International Journal of Career Management. Bradford: MCB University Press.

Journal of Occupational and Organisational Psychology. Leicester: BPS.

Journal of Vocational Behavior. San Diego, CA: Academic Press.

Newcheck. Sheffield: COIC.

Personnel. New York: AMA.

Personnel Management (Journal of the Institute of Personnel Management). London: IPM.

Personnel Review. Bradford: MCB University Press.

Training and Development (Journal of the Institute of Training and Development). Marlow: ITD.

Training and Development Journal. Alexandria, VA: ASTD.

Appendix H
Useful Organisations

British Association for Counselling (BAC)
1 Regent Place
Rugby
Warwickshire CV21 2PJ

British Psychological Society (BPS)
Occupational Psychology Section
St Andrews House
48 Princess Road East
Leicester LE1 7DR

Career Counselling Services
46 Ferry Road
London SW13 9PW

Careers and Occupational Information Centre (COIC)
St Mary's House
Moorfoot
Sheffield S1 4PQ

Careers Research and Advisory Centre (CRAC)
Sheraton House
Castle Park
Cambridge CB3 0AX

Counselling and Career Development Unit (CCDU)
University of Leeds
44 Clarendon Road
Leeds LS2 9PJ

Guidance Development Unit (GDU)
Employment Department
St Mary's House
Moorfoot
Sheffield S1 4PQ

Institute of Careers Guidance (ICG)
27a Lower High Street
Stourbridge
West Midlands DY8 1TA

Institute of Personnel Management (IPM)
Career Counselling and Outplacement Forum
Camp Road
Wimbledon
London SW19 4UX

Institute of Training and Development (ITD)
Marlow House,
Institute Road,
Marlow, Bucks SL7 1BD

National Institute of Careers Education and Counselling (NICEC)
Sheraton House
Castle Park
Cambridge CB3 0AX

National Council for Educational Technology (NCET)
Sir William Lyons Road
University of Warwick Science Park
Coventry CV4 7EZ

National Council for Vocational Qualifications (NCVQ)
222 Euston Road
London NW1 3BZ

Training Access Point (TAP) Unit
Employment Department
St Mary's House
Moorfoot
Sheffield S1 4PQ

References

Adams, J., Hayes, J. and Hopson, B. (1976) *Understanding and Managing Personal Change*. London: Martin Robertson.

Allen, C.A. (1975) 'Life planning: its purpose and position in the human potential movement'. MA thesis, University of Leeds.

Allport, G.W., Vernon, P.E. and Lindsey, G. (1960) *Study of Values: A Scale for Measuring the Dominant Interests in Personality*. Boston, MA: Houghton Mifflin.

Anastasi, A. (1988) *Psychological Testing*. New York: Macmillan.

Arthur, M.B., Hall, D.T. and Lawrence, B.S. (eds) (1989) *Handbook of Career Theory*. Cambridge: Cambridge University Press.

Bailey, C. (1982) *Beginning in the Middle*. London: Quartet Books.

Ball, B. (1984) *Careers Counselling in Practice*. Brighton: Falmer Press.

Berne, E. (1968) *Games People Play*. Harmondsworth: Penguin.

Betz, N. and Fitzgerald, L.F. (1987) *The Career Psychology of Women*. New York: Academic Press.

British Association for Counselling (1990) *Code of Ethics and Practice for Counsellors*. Rugby: BAC.

British Association for Counselling (1992) *Counselling and Psychotherapy Resources Directory*. Rugby: BAC.

Clarkson, P. (1989) *Gestalt Counselling in Action*. London: Sage.

Clay, J. (1989) *Men at Midlife: The Facts, the Fantasies, the Future*. London: Sidgwick and Jackson.

Collin, A. (1979) 'Mid-life crisis and its implications in counselling', *British Journal of Guidance and Counselling*, 7(2): 144–52.

Dail, H.L. (1989) *The Lotus and the Pool: How to Create Your Own Career*. Boston, MA: Shambhala Publications.

Dryden, W. (1979) 'Rational-emotive therapy and its contribution to careers counselling', *British Journal of Guidance and Counselling*, 7(2): 181–7.

Edwards, R. (1989) *Separating Educational and Vocational Guidance*. National Association of Educational Guidance Services. Occasional publication.

Egan G. (1990) *The Skilled Helper: Model, Skills and Methods for Effective Helping*, 4th edn. Monterey, CA: Brooks/Cole.

Ellis, A. (1962) *Reason and Emotion in Psychotherapy*. New York: Lyle Stuart.

Erikson, E. (1971) *Identity: Youth and Crisis*. London: Faber and Faber.

Floyed, J. and Nathan, R. (1991) *The CCS Job Hunting Manual*. London: Career Counselling Services.

Francis, D. (1985) *Managing Your Own Career*. London: Collins.

Harren, V.A. (1974) 'A model of career decision-making for college students', *Journal of Vocational Behaviour*, 14: 119–33.

Hawkins, P. and Shohet, R. (1989) *Supervision in the Helping Professions*. Milton Keynes: Open University Press.

Hawthorn, R. (1991) *Who Offers Guidance*. Sheffield: Employment Department.

Heron, J. (1990) *Helping the Client: A Creative Practical Guide*. London: Sage.

Herriot, P. (1992) *The Career Management Challenge: Balancing Individual and Organisational Needs*. London: Sage.

Hess, A.K. (ed.) (1980) *Psychotherapy Supervision: Theory, Research and Practice*. New York: Wiley.

Holland, J.L. (1983) *Making Vocational Choices: A Theory of Careers*. Englewood Cliffs, NJ: Prentice-Hall.

Hopson, B. and Scally, M. (1991) *Build Your own Rainbow: a Workbook for Career and Life Management*. Leeds: Lifeskills Associates.

Inskipp, F. (1988) *Counselling Skills*. Cambridge: National Extension College.

Jackson, C. (1990) *Careers Counselling in Organisations: The Way Forward*. IMS Report 198. Sussex: Institute of Manpower Studies.

Killeen, J.F. and Kidd, J.M. (1991) *Learning Outcomes of Guidance: A Review of Recent Research*. Sheffield: Employment Department.

Lemmer, E.M. (1991) 'Untidy careers: occupational profiles of re-entry women', *International Journal of Career Management*, 3(1): 9–15.

Levinson, D.J., Darrow, C., Klein, E., Levinson, M. and McKee, B. (1978) *The Seasons of a Man's Life*. New York: Knopf.

London, M. and Stumpf, S.A. (1982) *Managing Careers*. New York: Addison-Wesley.

Mael, F.A. (1991) 'Desire for career upward mobility and workplace adaptation', *International Journal of Career Management*, 3(4): 10–16.

Megranahan, M. (1989) *Counselling: A Practical Guide for Employers*. London: Institute of Personnel Management.

Moreland, J.R. (1979) 'Some implications of life-span development for counseling psychology', *Personnel and Guidance Journal*, 57: 299–304.

Mulligan, J. (1988) *The Personal Management Handbook*. London: Sphere.

Nathan, R. and Floyed, J. (1991) *The CCS Self-Assessment Manual*. London: Career Counselling Services.

Nathan, R. and Syrett, M. (1983) *How to Survive Unemployment: Creative Alternatives*. Harmondsworth: Penguin.

Nelson-Jones, R. (1991) *Lifeskills: A Handbook*. London: Cassell Educational.

Newland Park Associates (1991) *Review of Psychometric Tests for Assessment in Vocational Training*. Leicester: British Psychological Society.

Oakeshott, M. (1991) *Educational Guidance for Adults: Identifying Competencies*. Further Education Unit.

Offer, M. (ed.) (1991a) *The Careers Software Review*. Coventry: National Council for Educational Technology.

Offer, M. (1991b) *An Introduction to the Use of Computers in Guidance*. Sheffield: Guidance Development Unit.

Parsons, F. (1909) *Choosing a Vocation*. Boston, MA: Houghton-Mifflin.

Proctor, B. (1988) *Supervision: A Working Alliance* (Videotape Training Manual). St Leonards on Sea: Alexia Publications.

Roberts, K. (1981) 'The sociology of work entry and occupational choice', in A.G. Watts, D. Super and J. Kidd (eds) *Career Development in Britain*. Cambridge: CRAC/Hobsons.

Rogers, C. (1965) *On Becoming a Person*. London: Constable.

Rowan, J. (1989) *Subpersonalities: The People Inside Us*. London: Routledge.

Schein, E.H. (1978) *Career Dynamics: Matching Individual and Organisational*

Needs. New York: Addison-Wesley.

Schuller, T. and Walker, A. (1990) *The Time of Our Life: Education, Employment and Retirement in the Third Age*. Institute for Public Policy Research/Employment Paper 2.

Sheehy, G. (1976) *Passages: Predictable Crises of Adult Life*. London: Bantam.

Shepherd, R. (ed.) (1991) *CIOLA Directory: The Adviser's Guide to Careers Information Resources*. Cambridge: Careers Research and Advisory Centre.

Skills and Enterprise Network (1991) *Labour Market and Skill Trends*. Sheffield: Employment Department.

Smith, M. (1989) *The Best is Yet to Come: a Workbook for the Middle Years*. Sheffield: Lifeskills Associates.

Stewart, I. (1989) *Transactional Analysis Counselling in Action*. London: Sage.

Sue, D.W. and Sue, D. (1990) *Counselling the Culturally Different*, 2nd edn. New York: Wiley.

Super, D.E. (1957) *The Psychology of Careers*. New York: Harper.

Super, D.E. (1980) 'A life-span, life-space approach to career development', *Journal of Vocational Behaviour*, 16: 282–98.

Taylor, N.B. (1985) 'How do career counsellors counsel?', *British Journal of Guidance and Counselling*, 13(2): 166–77.

Thomas, R.M. (1990) *Counseling and Life-Span Development*. Newbury Park, CA: Sage.

U.S. Department of Labor (1977) *Dictionary of Occupational Titles*, 4th edn. Washington, D.C.: U.S. Government Printing Office.

Whitmore, D. (1990) *Psychosynthesis Counselling in Action*. London: Sage.

Yost, E.B. and Corbishley, M.A. (1987) *Career Counselling: A Psychological Approach*. New York: Jossey-Bass.

Index